H. H. Sheneff .

Aug., 1939 .

THE QUEST FOR
RELIGIOUS CERTAINTY

THE QUEST
for
RELIGIOUS
CERTAINTY

by

HAROLD A. BOSLEY, Ph.D.

WILLETT, CLARK & COMPANY

CHICAGO   NEW YORK

1939

Copyright 1939 by
WILLETT, CLARK & COMPANY

Manufactured in The U.S.A. by The Plimpton Press
Norwood, Mass.-La Porte, Ind.

CONTENTS

PREFACE

SECULARISM, compounded as it is of the glorification of life, vaguely conceived, even pantheistically idealized, and of reverence for science as the farthest outreach and the most unshakable demonstration of human powers, has suffered irreparable damage within the last decade. The stress laid in recent scientific theory on the notion of indeterminism at the very heart of the universe has been as difficult for secularism as for religion to absorb. As a result of economic, political and international developments in the past decade secularism's confidence in man is in a much worse condition than religion's belief in God has ever been.

Secularism is on its way out. This, I think, most thoughtful observers would admit. But the admission must not be construed to mean that religion is on its way back. The emergence of religion as a dominant factor in personal life and in world affairs will not come about automatically. The factors which loosened its hold on the modern world are still at work: its failure to come to terms with either the conclusions or the method of science; its inability to find an effective ally in the field of contemporary philosophy; its utter neglect of the responsibility of clearly delineating and forcefully presenting ideals and values as patterns for the ordering of personal and social confusion; its failure to produce a philosophy of religion sufficiently comprehensive in scope to integrate in one vast, meaningful synthesis the wealth and richness of human life.

The damage wrought by seven hundred years of constant

disintegration is not going to be repaired by a book or a man or a generation. What I have tried to do in the following pages is no more than to present a humble introduction to the problem of certainty which thinkers in the field of religion have no choice but to face.

Chapters I and II attempt to present a picture of contemporary confusion and indicate the various directions which men have taken in the past and are taking today in their search for certainty. Chapter III is an attempt to clarify the meaning and types of certainty which men seek for. I may say, parenthetically, that the first three chapters form simple reading for the specialist and make no requirements in equipment which the average layman cannot produce. Chapters IV, V and VI deal with the meaning of tentativeness and attempt to clarify the philosophical ground upon which it rests. These are dark and difficult areas. There have been few if any attempts to relate them to problems of religion, and I hold no brief for the finality of this effort. Chapter IV is a general introduction to the themes that are discussed in detail in the two ensuing chapters. Chapters V and VI are the most difficult sections of the book. They strive to get down to bedrock, and while they will be relatively easy reading for one who is versed in philosophy, the layman in philosophy will find them exacting. Yet it is my hope that even he, by paying careful attention both to principles and to illustrations, will be able to appreciate the importance and grasp the meaning of the themes discussed.* Chapter VII brings the analytical discussion of the four preceding chapters to bear upon the problem of the nature of religious

---

* Two excellent recent works in the field of probability should be added to the ones referred to in Chap. V: Hans Reichenbach, *Experience and Prediction* (University of Chicago Press, 1938); Ernst Nagel, *Principles of the Theory of Probability* (University of Chicago Press, soon to be released).

beliefs. Chapters VIII, IX and X present the framework of a philosophy of religion based upon the investigations conducted in the preceding chapters.

I am indebted to the following publishers for permission to quote from volumes which have appeared under their imprint: Allen and Unwin, London; D. Appleton-Century Company; Doubleday, Doran and Company; the Encyclopedia Britannica; Harper and Brothers; the Macmillan Company; Minton, Balch and Company; G. P. Putnam's Sons; Oxford University Press; Charles Scribner's Sons; the University of Chicago Press; Yale University Press.

Instructors, classmates, colleagues and students of mine have all had a hand in making imperative and unavoidable the investigations and conclusions presented in these pages. Several of the student secretaries at the Iowa State Teachers' College performed the clerical work in connection with the manuscript, and I am especially grateful to Miss Marjorie Hovey, Mr. Armin Graber, Mr. Stanley Benz and Mr. James Stineheart. Two of my colleagues at that institution, Miss Katherine Buxbaum and Miss Alison Aitchison, gave generously of their time, and the reader profits by their kind criticism in many different ways. I cannot refrain from mentioning my deep indebtedness to the late professor of philosophy of the Nebraska Wesleyan University, Edward R. Lewis. Through four years, he proved himself to me and to all students a brilliant teacher, a constructive thinker, a kind but incisive critic and a warmly generous friend.

H. A. B.

Mount Vernon Place Methodist Church
Baltimore, Maryland

THE QUEST FOR
RELIGIOUS CERTAINTY

THE QUEST FOR CERTAINTY

CONTEMPORARY confusion in Christianity has increased to the point of bedlam over this matter of certainty. Two truisms account for the turmoil. The first is that our religious tradition has organized itself, historically speaking, around several great certainties. And the second is that we have lost them; not completely, to be sure, but their towering truths mean more to the historian of Western culture than to bewildered persons facing life crises. In an age when persons and social orders alike face life crises it is inevitable that there should be yearning for that day when men could cry with the erstwhile blind man, "One thing I know!" Which is precisely the crux of our problem. What is it that we *know*, religiously speaking? It is cheap wit to reply that the one certainty of our time is that all things are relative. Yet that comes close to describing the atmosphere in which we all live.

The real depth of our confusion is revealed when we list some of the great assurances through which the Christian religion has, at different times, introduced unity, direction, and integrity into human life. Though all the rest of the world should slip into the sea of relativity, these truths were regarded as absolute and immutable. Christianity was defined in terms of them.

For several centuries the Christian was one who believed that Jesus was Lord and who associated himself with the community of believers. Creed, ritual and ethical code were simple and austere. Later, and owing to processes which the historian can trace with considerable accuracy, this basic certainty was expanded to include the theology and sacraments of the catholic church as necessary to salvation. The Protestant Reformation introduced a radical shift in this fundamental conviction. Taking the movement by and large, its basic thesis could be stated thus: The Christian is one who accepts the Bible as the inspired and inerrant Word of God, and orders his life accordingly. Protestant Christianity did not thereby forsake the doctrines of the catholic church but professed to retain only those that were grounded in Scripture. A further development has taken place during the past seventy-five years. The " simple-gospel " movement has centered attention upon a theme which inspired the various brotherhood movements among laymen during the latter part of the Middle Ages. Its motto has been, " Follow Jesus." When in doubt consult the Gospels. The rest of the Bible is important but of secondary value as compared to the records of the life of Jesus.

Now so long as any one of these great conceptions could be accepted as certain truth, the believer achieved a perspective on all the rest of life. He had something to " tie to," a reliable point of departure as well as a guiding thread through the labyrinth of experience.

It is a fair question whether we can get along without some great truths, certainly grasped, around which to organize life and culture. It is difficult to attach meaning and significance to the notion of personal or social direction and motivation without some secure presuppositions akin to the ancient assurances. Psychiatrists are returning to religion because their patients need a sense of complete confidence in standards of value calculated to restore mental health. Small wonder that these scientists are urging ministers of religion to desist from theological controversy and socio-political discussion and to pay strict attention to the "fundamentals of religion," namely, those ideas, practices and habits which usher the worshiper into a world of harmony and beauty and security.

Occasionally a social scientist shakes himself free from the rather morbid task of studying and describing the behavior of human groups long enough to ask: "What are the possible constructive consequences of our studies? What *should* people do? How *should* they act?" Such queries almost inevitably produce talk about "the great society" or some such ideal state in which all men everywhere have the totality of their activities and interests organized around some common goal. But the ill-fated utopias of yesteryears and the numerous conceptions of the Kingdom of God, varying all the way from an otherworldly heaven to a reign of justice and brotherhood among men on earth, rise up to testify that our fathers were unable to formulate a goal which could command more than partial allegiance.

Religionists may well regard the willingness of psychiatrists and social scientists to turn to religion when they step into the realm of ends, goals, ideals or standards of value, as a token of rebirth of spirituality *providing religion has something to offer on these matters*. We would do well to reread in the *Arabian Nights* the tale of the rich man who invited a starving beggar to his table and besought him to partake of delectable foods which he mentioned by name — only the table was bare. We who lament the low estate of religion should engrave on our memories how the beggar, tortured beyond endurance by this deception, laid low his host with a mighty blow. Even the most optimistic of us wonder whether religion can regain its feet as did the chastened host and produce a real meal that will satisfy real hunger.

To adopt a more familiar figure, the Christian religion once more has a chance to lead a bewildered civilization out of the wilderness into a promised land — but, along with the rest of the world, it also seems to have lost its sense of direction. Every church and theological seminary in Christendom is haunted by the query, " Can the blind lead the blind? "

Most of us will agree, I suppose, that the great religious certainties of yesterday are gone beyond recall. Although there is in them all a nub of abiding truth which may be salvaged after critical examination, it is unlikely that any serious attempt can or will be made to reinstate them *in toto* in the contemporary world. To recognize this probability is neither to disparage the ancient formulations as " old-fashioned " or " outmoded " nor to laud the modern world as progressive. It means, simply and solely, that during the past two centuries altogether too many revolutions have occurred in every area of culture for us ever to derive emotional peace and a sense of security from formulations of faith with which an earlier time was comfortably satisfied. The basic life patterns of the cultural epochs in terms of which Christianity stated the fundamentals of its faith are irrevocably broken. These life patterns furnished the soil within which the emotional life of their day was organized, and when religion sank the roots of its beliefs into them, certainty resulted.

The processes of history may be cyclic, as Spengler argues, but one of the glorious torments of human beings is that we who live in a later cycle can know and partially appreciate what has gone before. No amount of needing, hoping or praying can restore the culture patterns in terms of which Paul stated his flaming faith. Christianity is now seen to be a historical movement which has always stated its fundamental faith in terms of the thought patterns of each distinctive age. The most disturbed and confused periods in this movement have been those when Christianity moved from one cultural sea into another — rather, perhaps, when it left one environment for another, as did those species of marine life which became land animals. In this perspective doctrines are seen to be mortal things growing by adaptation to environment, with many unable to survive changing conditions.

Two other reasons for the present depreciation of Christianity deserve a hearing. First, the ancient assurances of the Christian religion have fallen afoul of each other, not historically alone, but within our time. Take the hoary controversy between faith and works as related to salvation. This, I take it, describes the radical difference which separates Barthians from exponents of the social gospel. Yet each of the parties to the controversy is willing to stake the very meaning and existence of God on the accuracy of his position. The Barthians say: If God be not above this howling chaos of existence, above even human concepts, then he is only a convenient fiction inflated to cosmic proportions in order to sanctify some social scheme or other. The social gospel folk are equally decisive. They declare: If God is not actively operative within as well as beyond the ferment of our day, then he is not only unknowable but exactly useless — he doesn't exist so far as human problems are concerned.

Nor are faith and works the only Christian certainties of other days which are locked in this internecine struggle. Faith and reason continue to defy our best efforts to put them in double harness. The church and the Bible as sources of certainty do not dwell together in harmony. So it goes throughout the entire range of Christian truths. It is clear that they enjoyed their respective periods of power when they were related to thought and culture patterns which have now passed and cannot be recalled. The social consequences of the controversy are vivid and tragic. Our day, burdened with churches and theologies staking their all on some one certainty or other, is feeling the full force of the fierce differences which have riven the Christian tradition from its very inception. Small wonder that we find Catholics striving to clarify the meaning of " Catholic Action " and Protestants searching for a " new social strategy."

Nor should we ignore the neglected state of the rites and customs through which central Christian convictions have manifested themselves in society. The practices of religion, such as consistent fellowship in the community of believers, public and private worship, interest in the sacraments and conviction as to their importance, are misunderstood and neglected to a point that calls forth acute alarm, if one may judge by the breath-taking proposals calculated to restore their pre-eminence. Roger Babson would promote consistent fellowship in the community of believers by luring tired moderns once a week into a service whose appeal rests on the twin virtues of brevity and of absence of theological and socially radical preaching. So far as I know, however, no one has offered an equally " convincing " solution to the problem of the almost complete neglect of private and family worship as well as of participation in the accepted sacraments of any particular church. When both the intellectual substructure of a given belief and the practice which it validates collapse, what is left is a mound of ruins, of interest to one who wants imaginatively to reconstruct the life of other days rather than to one who is looking for a home.

The other reason for the vanishing of our inherited certainties is the long overdue recognition of the facts that Christianity is only one among many great world religions; that not one of the religions that live today goes back much beyond 1000 B.C.; that all the world religions, dead and living alike, have throbbed with great though different certainties. To be sure, the human needs which underlie these religions are continuous and the same, but the certainties which make a religion vital have to do with solutions aimed to meet these needs. Hence we today must recognize that not only are our Christian certainties dependent for their power upon attachment to some vanished historical epoch but, in addition, that Christianity is a movement within a segment of the human race which is relatively small temporally, numerically and geographically, and that other religions have proposed other certainties to the rest of mankind.

It is high time to raise the question: What price certainty? Is it as important as we have pretended? May not the search for it simply be an evasion of the insecurities inevitable to growth, an endeavor to " freeze " the map of life at a given stage wherein the basic needs of the group crying for certainty are at least partially met? These questions cannot fairly be disposed of as a case of sour grapes. Sociologists are recognizing that the desire for new experience, for adventure, is as basic to human life as the craving for security. Agathon demands of Socrates that he visualize a state comprehensive enough to provide for divine discontent, the restless searchings of men; anything else will be less a state than a sty.

Life is a hazardous process at best — one in which losses are as real and crushing as victories are actual and sweet; one in which our desires can set us on the search for solutions, yet can force neither their discovery nor eventuation. Some solutions work, others do not. Our prime concern is the satisfaction of felt needs, however we may define them. I take it that few will seriously contend that we have satisfied this concern today. An exaggerated concern for certainty can crush out or minimize the desire for new experience in a crisis when, in the interest of seeking more satisfactory solutions, we need above all else the willingness to " break new seas." John Dewey's *The Quest for Certainty* furnishes indisputable evidence for this statement. He shows how philosophy and religion alike have defended by argument and enshrined in doctrine a conception of man and nature which was calculated to give a feeling of cognitive and emotional certainty at the price of actual security. Men bowed before nature when what was needed was investigation and manipulation of natural forces to the end of meeting human needs. The only significant certainty, Dewey argues, is that which derives from genuine security.

I for one am willing to grant that we have overstressed the extent to which religion needs certainty. I do not mean to imply that certainty is unessential, only that it is not the whole of our need. Religious leaders are all too likely to cry, " Certainty, certainty, we must have certainty," without pausing to ask what it is or why it is so essential. It is doubtful whether any other area of human thought can produce so many shining examples of mésalliances between good intentions and bad arguments as that of religion's quest for certainty. The utterly distressing feature of our contemporary endeavors is that they resemble a mad scramble rather than an orderly expedition. Definitions are vague, logic is tenuous, and the conclusions are acceptable only to those who are willing to grasp at the proverbial straws.

Nor have the critics of Christianity been any more intelligent in their approach to this problem. There is, I believe, no more eloquent indication of the true extent of intellectual panic in religion than Walter Lippmann's treatment of certainty in his *A Preface to Morals*. This masterpiece of clarity on most issues and of complete candor on all, without even attempting a definition of certainty begins by pointing out that we no longer have it and why. This, Mr. Lippmann argues, is where modern religion fails, because " without complete certainty religion does not offer genuine consolation. . . . Without certainty there can be no profound sense that a man's own purpose has become part of the purpose of the whole creation." [1] I do not mean to suggest that the author's conclusions would have been different had he first defined with care the crucial concept; but I must insist that as the matter stands, no one, not even Mr. Lippmann, knows precisely what it is he is discussing.

This chapter will have served its purpose if it calls attention to (1) religion's embarrassment when it must confess to a seeking world that its historic certainties have been shaken and cannot be re-established; (2) the fact that our frantic search for certainty has resulted in overemphasizing its importance to life as a whole; (3) the woeful lack of precision as to the meaning of certainty and the importance of it, whatever it does mean.

It is now time to leave the area of general charges and produce some concrete examples of the chaotic tendencies of contemporary Christian thought in regard to the quest for religious certainty.

[1] *A Preface to Morals* (New York: The Macmillan Co., 1929), pp. 49 f.

PRESENT DIRECTIONS OF THE QUEST

NOT WITHOUT a struggle, at least not without a cry of protest, has the modern world reacted to the crumbling of ancient certainties, "the dissolution of the ancestral pattern." Contemporary thinkers are accepting the challenge and the work of reconstruction is being pushed on all sides. One fact is obvious: we are determined to have certainty somewhere, somehow. A brief historical survey of one aspect of Western culture will reveal one reason behind our determination.

The Western intellect has traveled for the past two millennia on three great truthward roads.[1] Philosophy provided the first highway, and for almost eight centuries the only one. Theology then displaced philosophy and determined the journey for twelve centuries. Some three hundred years ago a new but widening and promising way was opened up by science, and traveling it has proved to be an exacting and rewarding adventure.

Though these three roads lay through widely differing terrains they were alike in one significant respect: each guaranteed certainty to him who would accept its discipline and keep his feet on the designated pathway. This point of agreement is, I think, the clue to our refusal to accept as final the disintegration of the bases of certainty. A somewhat fuller description of the way each discipline achieved certainty — or,

[1] William Minto, *Logic, Inductive and Deductive* (New York: Charles Scribner's Sons, 1915), p. 14.

to be more exact, its method of determining truth — will throw considerable light on certain tendencies in the contemporary way of meeting the situation.

PHILOSOPHY'S ROAD TO TRUTH

This, said classical philosophy, is the way to reach truth, and gain that certainty which is essential to stability and security: Recognize that the truth of any proposition is determined by its coherence with a set of first principles. Although this criterion sounds harmless enough, when you begin to examine its implications you run straightway into the point that the most worth-while thing in life is something *outside* of the experiences of living. Goodness is valuable not because it is encountered in experience, but because the good is the apex of a set of philosophical first principles which come to be that which confers importance upon individual acts of goodness. It would be a mistake to lump all the classical philosophies together and say that they agreed upon the fundamental nature of these first principles, but their most powerful formative minds, Plato and Aristotle, firmly adhered to the position that the most important fact in life is not the ebb and flow of daily experience but a system of first principles which reach beneath change and seize the essence or the form of change, and thereby determine what things are and what things are not valuable.

This, of course, was wholly an affair of the intellect. Religion's endeavor to guide man to supreme values through ritual and faith had little or no place in this scheme of things. In those far-off days men thought that their endowment with mind put them in possession of an instrument trusty enough to probe the heart of the universe. Hence the unconscionable emphasis upon the metaphysical nature of ideas. Reality came to be conceived as a series of logical propositions, a set of mutually consistent ideas, and the ebb and flow of daily experience received scarcely a civil greeting. We have ample reason to believe that not for a single moment did these virile folk think that life as they lived it from day to day was any such abstraction; yet they were willing to stake their all on the proposition that the universe in which they lived was basically such an ideational arrangement. And in all fairness we must reckon these eight hundred years from Plato to Augustine among the most fruitful in the career of the Western mind. Brilliant insights, daring generalizations and dazzling speculations combine with an acute appreciation of the commonplace to make of classical philosophy a perpetual fire for burning dross and impurities from the mind of man.

THEOLOGY'S QUEST FOR TRUTH

But philosophy for all its merits and strength finally yielded its position to the new religion of Christianity, which in its inception had no unduly exalted estimate of the importance of the human intellect. Paul's letters are all too tart on this point. He points out that God finds it easier to work through the ignorance of the ignorant than through the wisdom of the wise and that all the long disputations over the fine points of philosophic systems had gained the heated debaters precisely nothing. Having thus branded philosophy's road to truth as the way to perdition, the Christian religion presented its own conception of the way certainty could be attained. Hence theology arose to explain and defend the Christian road to truth.

The fundamental principle of theology may sound suspiciously like that of philosophy. But while there is much in common between the two points of view, it will be apparent almost at once that an unbridgeable chasm yawns between them. The fundamental assumption of Christian theology is this: The truth of a proposition is determined by its coherence with revealed truth, i.e., with dogmas. I have no intention of getting into a wrangle over religious dogmas if it can be avoided. I feel with Sir Edmund Gosse in his delightful autobiography, *Father and Son,* that it is a fine thing to let sleeping dogmas lie. But in this connection we must disturb them.

Augustine, one of the earliest theologians of first rank, was a skilled philosopher before he became a Christian; that is to say, he had acquired a profound respect for the human intellect as well as a deep distrust of its ability to answer all or any of the fundamental questions which might be asked of life and the universe. Some of the other great contributors to Christian theology in its earliest days were as deeply dyed in philosophy as Augustine, so we must be prepared for a distinction which will recognize the value and validity of the human intellect up to a certain point and prohibit it from meddling beyond that mark. This is precisely the position which Christian theology took from the day of Augustine down to that of Thomas Aquinas, who gave it its classic form.

According to this division, there are two types of religion: rational, in which the human mind has full and complete freedom; revealed, before which the eyes of the mind must quietly close in deepest reverence. Of course the most important things all came, sooner or later, to be connected with revealed religion in the form of dogmas. Every fundamental concept in Christianity found itself in the area of revealed religion either as doctrine or as dogma, understanding by these, formulations of central truths not only sustained by the entire structure of theology but also vouchsafed by the church. The freedom extended to the human mind contained the proviso that it be not diverted from this roadway. Scholasticism resolutely insisted that human reason can reach a knowledge of God under its own power. Yet this affirmation is continually dwarfed by the towering assertion that the source of indubitable certainty in the area of truth is that of revealed dogma.

In fact, many a luckless thinker was dubbed a heretic because his intellectual processes did not lead him into the arms of revealed religion with as much rapidity as his brethren thought they should. These were the glorious days when men knew the answer to every important question. That age of supreme certainty and security lasted for almost twelve hundred years, down to the time of Francis Bacon in the sixteenth and early seventeenth centuries. Within this long span of time there were many thinkers like Abélard whose reflections led them almost to the brink of denying the fundamental nature of revealed religion, but without exception they shrank back from the awful void into which they gazed.

SCIENCE'S SEARCH FOR TRUTH

During the sixteenth and seventeenth centuries there arose a new movement which manifested as much vitality and promise as had Christianity in its earliest days. This was modern science. Quickly its promises and achievements injected a growing dissatisfaction into the erstwhile earnest followers of theology. Science indicated another road to truth: that the truth of a proposition is determined by its coherence with empirical data — with things, if you please. The world of trees, sticks, stones, people, and all observable objects was finally acknowledged to be the seedbed of truth, and every idea which claimed to be true had to present grubby, earthy evidence of its validity. No philosophical or theological postulate would suffice; it had to have the facts before it could get a hearing. It is easy to understand why Francis Bacon, as prophet of the new movement, should inveigh so bitterly against classical philosophy and theology. It was from these barren roads that the new movement had rescued the human mind. For a period of more than two hundred years it seemed as though the human mind under the discipline of scientific method would rifle the universe of all her secrets. The eighteenth and nineteenth centuries were preeminently characterized by intensity of research in every conceivable direction. The human intellect applied itself with complete abandon to the physical, biological and social sciences. Philosophers and theologians still argued and wrangled among themselves, but the number of persons interested in what they had to say was rapidly decreasing.

Sensitive spirits among the poets first realized that a subtle but disastrous change had come into the cultural climate.[2] Goethe, Wordsworth and Matthew Arnold, to mention only three, began to call attention to the fact that while the human mind was achieving one great success after another in the field of various researches, the human spirit was dying. Man's sense of cultural continuity, of his real dependence upon the work and ideas of men who lived in antiquity, was dimmed to the point of darkness. And the poets summed up their charge this way: If we must give up our sense of humility in the presence of achievements of past generations, if we must sacrifice the rich world accessible only to imagina-

---

[2] So far as I know, A. N. Whitehead was the first thinker to give credit to the poets for this accomplishment.

tion, if the outreaches of the spirit in the form of religion are to be rejected as superstition — if this is the price we are asked to pay for the admitted benefits of science, then it is too high.

But the cry of the poets was brushed aside as so much romantic nonsense, and the human mind continued its hard, rewarding labors along the highway of science. For when science laid down its fundamental postulate decreeing that truth is determined by coherence with things, the world of spiritual values, upon which religion and poetry were based, was necessarily regarded as an illusion. It was during this stressful period that thinkers began to distinguish between facts and values, assigning science to the area of facts and religion to the area of values. This distinction aimed to rescue the prerogatives of art and religion from attrition caused by science. But the hoped-for relief did not come from this source.

This third journey was the shortest one of all, lasting from the days of Francis Bacon in the seventeenth century to the time of Boutroux, Peirce and Whitehead, who began to make their famous criticisms of scientific theory in the latter part of the nineteenth century. Science could neither laugh off nor set aside as romantic nonsense their question: What are these " things " about which you speak when you say that truth is determined by coherence with " things " or empirical data of " things "? So long as scientific theory could fall back upon the notion that the atom possessed a certain intrinsic being as the element to which all the rest of physical matter could be reduced (Newton held this), the answer was fairly clear. But when scientific research began to break the atom up into more and more infinitesimal units which derive their significance more from action than from location, it seemed as though the universe itself had taken sides against the fundamental postulate of science. To this very day and hour no one is quite sure how to answer the questions: What is "matter"? What are "things" anyway? What possible meaning inheres in the formula that truth is discovered through consistency with "things"?

Suffice it to say that the layman's undivided regard for science was interrupted by several appalling consequences of the practical application of science. Outstanding among these was the World War. Men began to call science a "false Messiah." [3] The whole movement of literary humanism amounts to nothing less than a repudiation of the fundamental postulate with which science had begun in the sixteenth and seventeenth centuries.

These considerations help us to account for the fact that we no longer tread with confidence the roadway of science. We are, to be sure, free to walk in almost any direction, but simply to strike out for the sake of going is gloomy business, as Krutch demonstrates. [4]

Since man has become accustomed to the comfortable claim of possessing some form of certainty, it is not surprising to find the thinkers of our day anxiously endeavoring to attain it in one way or another. This endeavor is not peculiar to religion, but is characteristic as well of philosophy, [5] art [6] and scientific theory. [7] However, our attention

[3] C. E. Ayres, *Science, the False Messiah* (Indianapolis: Bobbs-Merrill Co., 1927).

[4] Joseph W. Krutch, *The Modern Temper* (New York: Harcourt, Brace & Co., 1930).

[5] John Dewey, *Reconstruction in Philosophy* (New York: Henry Holt & Co., 1920); H. A. Overstreet, *We Move in New Directions* (New York: W. W. Norton Co., 1933).

[6] Krutch, *Experience and Art* (New York: R. R. Smith, 1932); Dewey, *Art as Experience* (New York: Minton, Balch & Co., 1935).

[7] P. W. Bridgman, *The Logic of Modern Physics* (New York: The Macmillan Co., 1927).

will be confined to the area of religion.[8] Our immediate task, then, is briefly to indicate four specific insights and two systems which are receiving considerable attention because they promise new pathways to certainty.

1. "High Religion." This, especially as expounded by Walter Lippmann, is probably the most popular movement among sober sophisticates. It begins by pointing out, as we saw in earlier pages, that traditional religion is decadent because its great certainties are no longer compelling. The reason for this falling off was the discovery that these certainties were in large measure projected fulfillments of uncriticized desires. We wanted security here and hereafter; hence we demanded assurances regarding God and immortality, among other things, which would vouchsafe our fond but extravagant desires. The way out is to scale our desires down to reality. We must learn to want only what we can have. This requires an enormous amount of courage and the highest type of spiritual discipline. Hence Walter Lippmann regards this position as one of "high religion." Science and tradition can help us determine what the universe will permit; intelligence and fortitude will aid us in seeking these possibilities. Certainty for "high religion" then amounts to accepting the fact that one will want only what is within the area of possible achievement.

The complicated catch in this endeavor is, first, how to know what things are possible, and, second, how to keep our desires confined thereto. The frontiers of possibility move back with amazing rapidity and often without forewarning. The devotee of "high religion" can, to be sure, strike his

----

[8] E. E. Aubrey, *Present Theological Tendencies* (New York: Harper & Bros., 1936). This I regard as the clearest exposition of what is going on in contemporary Christian thought.

tents and follow after. If he recognizes the likelihood of new possibilities, then a place should be made for it as an integral aspect of his religion. But even " high religion " is not immune to the perpetual danger which dogs those who follow frontiers — mirages, the projection of desired and needed ends as truths certain enough to live by and, if necessary, to die for.

2. *Revelation.* After a two hundred year rest in the sequestered home of theology the concept of revelation is once more active in the marts of everyday thought. One of the most challenging theological movements of our day regards it as the crucial concept in religious reconstruction. I refer, of course, to the dialectical theology of Germany, which has begun to filter into England and America. For this movement, Christian Scriptures, theology and institutions are quite unintelligible apart from the controlling and luminous influence of revelation. Karl Barth asserts that Christians must accept the Bible as the Word of God and Jesus as the Son of God whose divine love condemns us as sinners yet promises salvation through faith. Carefully note: these are not rational assurances. They so bristle with contradictions that reason is unable to validate them, much less reach them. They come to us clothed with authority; they are messages and meanings sent of God.

We need not enter further into this provocative theology. Our present concern is to understand, if possible, precisely what is meant by revelation. Despite the warnings of Barth and his followers that reason must keep hands off we are entitled to observe that the concept is a part of our language and therefore has some connotations that ought to be intelligible to everyone. Several such are evident.

In the first place, some light is thrown upon the concept

when we realize that revelation takes precedence over all
that men can do, think and feel. Not only takes precedence,
but actually dismisses human experience as devoid of positive value. Professor Wilhelm Pauck, a friendly critic of
Barthianism, makes an illuminating comment on the background of this theological movement: "It is the old, old
question of certainty which is in the background of the
Barthian theology. That man cannot depend upon himself,
upon his human experiences, when this need is aroused —
this is the discovery in which Barth rejoiced when he wrote
his commentary on the Epistle to the Romans." [9]

Emil Brunner is particularly outspoken in his laudation
of revelation. For him it is *the* avenue of reliable knowledge. When someone demands that revelation give evidence
of its validity, Brunner replies that it cannot be done precisely because the truths of revelation cannot be stated in
terms calculated to coerce reason.[10] One must have faith
in revelation before its deliverances are compelling. When
one has such faith, his questions cease. For example: "The
real Christ is not visible to the historian's eye. To see the
revelation of God in Christ is a gracious privilege of faith,
of the believer and not of the historian; or metaphysically
speaking, the organ with which Christ is apprehended is not
the historian's scientific eye but the spiritual eye of the believer." [11]

Reason has a negative value; its rigorous exercise rewards
man just as the efforts of a fly to get off flypaper serve the fly
— he gets stuck all the tighter. Reason enables man to see

---

[9] Wilhelm Pauck, *Karl Barth* (New York: Harper & Bros., 1931), pp. 66 f.

[10] Emil Brunner, *The Theology of Crisis* (New York: Charles Scribner's Sons, 1929), pp. 37 ff.

[11] *Ibid.*, p. 42; cf. also Karl Barth, *The Word of God and the Word of Man* (Boston: Pilgrim Press, 1928), p. 277.

the profound contradictions which obtain between time and eternity, life and death, God and man. It likewise confesses its inability to resolve these contradictions, and with this confession man is stripped of his last pretension and stands naked before God awaiting his message.

Another important meaning of revelation is that it is a possible clue to the qualitative difference between God and man. Revelation always flows from God to man. By no amount of effort can man command a revelation. He can prepare himself to receive it, but that done he must wait. Revelation, then, is charged with a divine current with which it illuminates human life.[12] It proclaims unity and peace to man amid disunity and turmoil. God is seen as all-sufficient when man is deserted by every shred of self-sufficiency.

What criticism can be made of this road to truth? I do not see how we can avoid asserting that the logic by which certainty derives from revelation is unbreakable precisely because it ultimately forms a vicious circle. If one questions the validity of the claims made for revelation, he gets this answer: "As long as you remain an outsider, i.e., one who doubts revelation, you cannot verify its claims to absolute knowledge. To do this you must accept revelation, i.e., you must become an insider. You know you are an insider when you cease to doubt revelation." We can put the case for revelation in a single sentence: The only way you can resolve your doubts as to revelation is wholly to believe in it; when you wholly believe in it you will know that it is true.[13]

[12] Dr. E. G. Homrighausen warned me, in our first talk on these subjects, always to remember that revelation, for Barth, is dynamic, never static.

[13] H. H. Farmer, *The World and God* (New York: Harper & Bros., 1935). Chap. 5 presents a conception of revelation vastly different from that of dialectical theology.

3. *The Supernatural.* When science replaced theology as guide of the Western mind, one of the first traditional concepts to be discredited was that of the supernatural. Science knows no such area of reality — at least scientific method makes no provision for the perception of it. When science exercised unchallenged dominion, the whole notion of the supernatural was anathema to the educated mind. But science, as we have seen, is in a somewhat humbler mood these days. And one of the highways to certainty that is being indicated with increasing frequency is a form of supernaturalism. It is not simply a reaffirmation of the ancient form. Rather it aims to preserve the inherited values of the Christian tradition by a careful critique of science. This is commonly referred to as the "new supernaturalism."[14] Under the astute leadership of John Oman,[15] F. R. Barry[16] and H. H. Farmer,[17] it is a well knit theological system comprised of coherent metaphysical principles, a standard of ethical values, and doctrinal affirmations.

This movement indicts science on the grounds of method and conclusions alike. The method of science proceeds by analysis rather than by synthesis, by centering attention on the part rather than on the whole, by insisting that whatever is true must be mensurable. Its conclusions point to the existence of a world whose mass motion is explicable in terms of irrefragable law; a world of necessity rather than of freedom, one in which notions of value, ideal and "oughtness" have no relevance to conduct. This is the "natural" world disclosed by science.

But it is far from the whole story, argue these writers.

[14] Aubrey, *op. cit.,* chap. 5.
[15] *Natural and Supernatural* (New York: The Macmillan Co., 1931).
[16] *Christianity and the Modern World* (New York: Harper & Bros., 1932).
[17] *Op. cit.*

And they outline a theory of knowledge designed to place scientific procedure in its proper setting. John Oman, for example, distinguishes four types of knowing, the first two of which produce evidences of the supernatural while the last two (scientific knowing) yield the natural.[18] Perhaps a brief description of this epistemological scheme will make a little plainer why it is enjoying much favor now.

The first type of knowing — *awareness* — is the most inclusive. It is characterized by keen activity of all our senses. The whole of the environment is accepted. It is a perception of the wholeness of things. It does not know a particular object as object, but only as an object-in-its-context. The second type of knowing — *apprehension* — results when within the total field of awareness we single out some one thing while the rest of the field fades into a background, much as an orchestra forms a background for the soloist.

Comprehension is the third type of knowing and with it we enter into the domain controlled by science. It seeks further to isolate the individual item; and in order that we may interrogate it regarding its own private structure we allow the remainder of the original inclusive field of attention quietly and completely to disappear. At this juncture, *explanation,* the last type of knowing, takes full charge of the endeavor to discover the nature and purpose of the particular object.

Since the first two are the types of knowing which validate the existence and nature of what Oman calls " a peculiar kind of reality," we must try a little harder to get a precise picture of what goes on in them, especially in the first one.

A cross section of the state of awareness exhibits three dif-

---

[18] *Op. cit.,* pp. 120 ff. H. H. Farmer, *op. cit.,* chap. 2, uses the phrase " synthesizing intuition " to denote what Oman means by awareness and apprehension.

ferent kinds of qualities or characteristics. (1) There is a great variety and richness of sensation — sensory images of colors, odors, sounds, etc. None are detained and asked for passports, nor are they slighted in any way; they are simply and fairly received and no question arises as to possible illusions. This is possible because the perceiver is simply a sensitive plate on which his total environment is registering itself. (2) But we find more than sensory images in this state of awareness. Sensations are not helter-skelter but are in order and engender in the perceiving mind the consciousness of an objective unity of the whole. Objects are not isolated but are perceived in relations with other objects. But this perception of context is not a particular sensory image. In it we have the ingression of another order of datum, the import of which will be assessed in a moment. (3) From this symphony of the *whole* arises the music of meaning, not of parts, but of the totality. This is best described as the " undifferentiated holy," the reverence for the integrity of the environment. Hence we find poets, when they open their spirits to the rays of their total world, brooding over the sense of time, space and infinity. Surely, argues Oman, these products of the state of awareness are as real as the sensory perceptions but are not sensory data themselves. It may be said of them as of the Kantian categories, they arise *with* sensory data but are clearly different in kind or quality from them.

Thus we see that the last two characteristics inherent in the state of awareness constitute the evidence for the existence of a supernatural order of reality not independent of sensations but qualitatively different from them. Just as a friend is more than any list, however complete, of the sensory impressions which he produces, and as a poem is more than an array of metrical lines, so the deliverances of awareness are more than any list of sensory data.

This theory of knowledge, by virtue of which the relativities and necessities of nature are placed in the wider context of absolute and self-explanatory supernature, has been put to a wide and significant use by two other writers mentioned earlier. F. R. Barry [19] points out that the standard of ethical values is in the supernatural with its sense of absolute values or "valuation as sacred," to use Oman's phrase. Hence our ethical systems and moral codes are fingers pointing toward this area of ideal values and derive their importance therefrom. H. H. Farmer,[20] a pupil of Oman, writes an incisive book to show how the fundamental faith of the Christian religion in the reality of a warmly personal God is simply a further yet wholly consistent application of the theory of knowledge which we have just outlined.

If we can accept as valid this road to truth, then our quest for religious certainty is at an end. The state of awareness, this "synthesizing intuition" of environment, provides all that men have ever looked for under the name of religion. But this endeavor is only one of several types of intuitionism, and before we accept it we must reflect on the severe critique which can be made of the intuitional approach to reality. Since intuitionism is discussed in more detail in the next chapter, I shall do no more now than allude to it.

4. Value. During the past century increasing attention has been given to the area of values. Philosophy and theology have broken over boundaries which formerly kept them sharply separated and are now sharing an investigation in this field. Some of our most stimulating minds feel that patient research will discover the bases of certainty here if

[19] *Op. cit.*   [20] *Op. cit.*

anywhere. Thinkers as widely divergent on most matters as John Dewey, A. N. Whitehead, S. Alexander and Nicolai Hartmann agree that the acid test of their speculative enterprises is the question, What are the implications for human values?

Philosophers are analyzing the nature of meaning; psychologists are endeavoring to identify the experience of value in order to describe its nature; sociologists are investigating the nature of social experience and its value relationships; theologians are busy relating the results of these efforts to concrete problems of human needs. Astute critics like Walter Lippmann sense the fact that more than we like to admit in a time of confusion our ethical codes must become weaker instead of stronger until we discover a way of thinking about values compelling enough to control conduct. When we say that no one theory of value dominates the field of thought today, it is not alone to call attention to one of the most prolific sources of modern confusion, but also to indicate the vigor and intensity of the activity that characterizes the entire area.

The precise nature of certainty derived from the area of value depends, of course, upon the particular theory of value which one uses as a frame of reference. But for all theories of value this much is true: certainty is vouchsafed him who believes both in the reality of specific values and in the possibility of a fuller relationship with them. Beyond this I shall not now attempt to go, since in a later chapter [21] I shall indicate what impresses me as the most significant theory of value under consideration today.

Although modernism is largely a Protestant phenomenon, and Neo-Thomism a Roman Catholic movement, they agree

[21] Chap. VIII.

in reassigning certainty to Christian theology. A brief survey of the purpose and method of each will complete the present orientation of our quest.

Modernism. The purpose of modernism is "to lay hold on the vital spiritual insights of our Christian tradition and to make them intelligible to the modern mind."[22] The large assumption is that when these insights are intelligible they will once more vitalize society. Modernism is committed to the conviction that certainty (certain truths) sufficient for the direction of personal and social life is to be found in traditional Christian thought and practices, providing their basic meaning is expressed in contemporary terms and thereby related to existing problems. And it has, over the period of almost two hundred years, been fashioning a method for recapturing and once more putting into active service the truths embedded in doctrines fitted to other days.

The first half of the method is to see in any particular doctrine the human experiences, the social milieu, the emotional guarantees to person and group alike. Only in this way is it possible even approximately to discover why the formulation was meaningful. Without exception the "essence" of the insight clothes itself in analogies drawn from the period. Shailer Mathews has devoted an entire book[23] to the discussion of the various analogies used to express to succeeding generations the significance of Jesus' death. The patterns or analogies are more than figures of speech; they are, in addition, a reliable clue to the intensity with which the basic idea is held.

The second step in the method of this movement is to

[22] Aubrey, *op. cit.*, p. 24.
[23] *The Atonement and the Social Process* (New York: The Macmillan Co., 1930).

discover cultural tensions in our day similar to those in which the doctrines were vital. If such exist, then an analogy or symbol adequate to our mode of living must be found. For example, " sin " possessed a precise meaning when God was likened to a monarch and man to his subject. In this analogy sin was disobedience. If dictatorships continue to thrive, we may expect an increasing number of persons to understand this conception of sin. But, by and large, this particular pattern has lost its communicative value and we are looking for new analogies by which to explain what, in experience, corresponds to the concept. We squirm uneasily when someone speaks of a person as sinful but understand very clearly if the concept used is not sin but maladjustment. The latter concept carries a contemporary suggestion that touches off the meanings implicit in the basic insight.

For modernism, then, certainty continues to reside in Christian theology when this is seen to be the precipitate of group endeavor to release tensions and convey meanings via an analogy drawn from culture patterns.[24] Modernism likewise has confidence in its instrument, the historical method. Problems and doubts arise when even this method is unable to put a steady finger on the " essence " of theology. Yet the predication of certainty to theology is unwavering.

Neo-Thomism. Broadly speaking, the twin masters of Neo-Thomism are Aristotle and Aquinas. Its purpose is to recapture for society the basic unity which these great thinkers perceived to be immanent in the universe. Christian theology insistently affirms that God is the cosmic ground of unity. Neo-Thomism reasons that implicit in all em-

[24] The various books of Sydney Cave exemplify the modernist approach: *The Doctrine of the Person of Christ* (New York: Charles Scribner's Sons, 1925); *The Doctrines of the Christian Faith* (London: Hodder & Stoughton, 1931); *The Doctrine of the Work of Christ* (Nashville, Tenn.: Cokesbury Press, 1937).

pirical objects (a tree, for example) there is a spiritual principle, an entity, a form, to use Aristotle's expression. All such spiritual essences proceed from God, the Uncaused Cause. "Man, like every object in the world, has his nature, his essential quality, and also his activities. And man's essence, his soul, gives the body the perfection, the actual existence, its life." [25]

Theology has apprehended this basic truth in all areas or orders of creation. Therefore Neo-Thomism insists that the repository of indubitable truths, of certainty, is in Catholic theology. The method of perceiving it continues to be that of traditional theology, reason and faith, the former governed by valid inference, the latter by obedience to the authority of the church.

No more pressing task confronts Christian leaders than that of bringing some kind of genuine order out of this welter of conflicting attempts to achieve certainty. Our confusion will mount, not subside, until and unless we get a firm grasp on the fundamental truths by which we would reorder modern society. And the first step in this direction is to inquire with utmost care and fairness into the meaning of certainty, the various types of certainty, and the conditions and the extent to which it is possible for us to achieve certainty. The endeavor to do this will occupy the rest of these pages.

[25] Aubrey, *op. cit.*, pp. 137 f.

III

THE MEANING OF CERTAINTY

W E HAVE much to learn from the strategy with which pivotal philosophers have sought the meaning of certainty. Plato spends the greater part of the *Republic* showing that philosophers should direct the destinies of the ideal state. And this because the prime function of philosophy is to acquaint man with the idea of the good. Plato sums up the pregnant parable of the cave in these words: " My opinion is that in the world of knowledge the idea of good appears last of all, and is seen only with an effort; and, when seen, is also inferred to be the universal author of all things beautiful and right, parent of light and of the lord of light in this visible world, and the immediate source of reason and truth in the intellectual; and that this is the power upon which he who would act rationally either in public or private life must have his eye fixed."

It is easy to see why Plato feels that men who have laid hold of this idea of the good should direct the state. They are conscious of a relationship between man and his world which is reliable because it brings within the ken of man the most inclusive, enduring reality. Nor is this a matter of inarticulate intuitionism. Rather the good immediately relates itself to mundane affairs in the form of ethical concepts and beliefs. This is Plato's path to certainty.

Descartes seeks for certainty by doubting everything that can be doubted. When the skeptical scouring is completed he finds that he still possesses some "clear and distinct ideas." This is what he wants and all that he needs because, for him, these ideas represent an indisputably reliable relationship between himself and his world. His doubt of himself leads to a ringing affirmation not only of his own reality but also of the existence of God. The latter belief gains strength when Descartes finds that among his few "clear and distinct" ideas there is one about a "perfect being." The very fact that he possesses the idea, he concludes, reinforces the belief in the existence and the perfection of God. Given the twin concepts of self and God and a confidence in their reality, Descartes is able to deal *via mathematica* with the remainder of his problems.

Descartes and Plato share the conviction that it is possible for one "with effort" to achieve an indubitable experience of that which is most deeply true of the universe. They likewise agree that this experience can be profitably articulated in beliefs. Neither holds that such beliefs are photographic reproductions of reality, but rather that they provide a reliable sketch of it *at those points where human life touches it*.

John Dewey believes that the various quests for certainty can be best understood as endeavors to solve a single problem: " Man has beliefs which scientific inquiry vouchsafes, beliefs about the actual structure and processes of things, and he also has beliefs about the values which should regulate his conduct. The question of how these two ways of believing may most effectively and fruitfully interact with one another is the most general and significant of all the problems which life presents to us." [1]

Although *The Quest for Certainty* concludes that certainty

[1] *The Quest for Certainty* (New York: Minton, Balch & Co., 1929), pp. 18–19.

is unattainable, its author, in an earlier work, gives the reason why the search for it must and will continue: " Two things are equally inept. One is to forget that human nature must have something upon which to rest; the other is to fancy that one's own preferred foundation-stones are the only things that will bring stability and security to others." [2]

One thing is fairly clear in the basic problem as Dewey states it: Human nature cannot come to rest in " something " unless that " something " is regarded as bringing felt values into relationship with the processes of the universe as revealed by scientific inquiry. The several roads to certainty to be considered in the following pages all presuppose the reality of the value experience — the consciousness of value — and are advanced as ways of discovering the fuller nature of value in order to make possible more precise judgments regarding it. Our immediate problem is to secure a conception of certainty that can lend genuine assistance in the search for a way to bridge this chasm between felt values and the nature of reality, between the consciousness of value and reliable judgments of value. I am convinced that the definition we need in order to clarify our thinking at the beginning of the quest is implicit in the combined efforts of Plato, Descartes and Dewey, and can be formulated this way: Certainty is man's consciousness of a reliable relationship, stated in terms of belief, between himself and his world.

I wish first to point out that the definition includes within itself the various types of certainty that have been and are being sought. It is possible to place the emphases at various places in the formulation, and thinkers have done and are continuing to do this very thing. Some stress *man's consciousness* of his relationship to the world and are fortunate

[2] *Characters and Events* (New York: Henry Holt & Co., 1929), II, 453–54.

if they escape the nadir of subjectivism — solipsism. Others stress the *relationship* and search for ways of increasing its reliability. Still others swing to the extreme of objectivity and stress *the world and its characteristics,* purporting thereby to describe the nature of things. It is a difference of emphasis, and careful thinking must always reach out to the other factors regardless of the one which it uses as a point of departure. Whatever merit the definition may have derives from its endeavor to call attention to all three emphases, not as separate entities but as aspects of an organic whole.

Although I am insisting that the certainty which we seek is broader than any one type, it will none the less be instructive to survey the various kinds of certainty that have been sought. They can be classified in two pairs: (1) psychological and logical, (2) certainty of conclusion and certainty of method.

PSYCHOLOGICAL AND LOGICAL CERTAINTY

Morris Cohen tirelessly insists that certainty is either psychological or logical.[3] Psychological certainty stresses man's consciousness of something as being true. It is not a state of dispassionate awareness. It is what Charles Dinsmore calls " assured conviction." [4] It is not simple cognition; rather it is an idea which is the channel through which emotional security and peace flow. Certainty so conceived holds that a belief is validated by the intensity of one's feeling that it is true. On this basis Columbus, prior to his voyages to the Americas, was right when he felt that the earth was round because he was passionately convinced that it was round. But by the same token our Zionist friend, Voliva, is right

[3] *Reason and Nature* (New York: Harcourt, Brace & Co., 1931), pp. 83 ff.

[4] *Religious Certitude in an Age of Science* (Chapel Hill, N. C.: University of North Carolina Press, 1924), p. 74.

when he asserts that the earth is flat because he is so firmly convinced that it is flat that he is willing to pay money to anyone who can convince him otherwise.

Obviously there is no possible disproof of a belief so held. Each man's belief stands uncontradicted and uncontradictable in his sight. The method by which he holds it is not amenable either to proof or to disproof due to external changes. Waxing and waning of emotional intensity alone determine the fluctuations in the status of the belief. Knowledge comes to stand for the sum total of what men passionately believe to be true. Beyond this we cannot go nor should we have any desire to go. There is no check on knowledge, no way to determine what is more and what less certain. The concept "verification" would drop out of our vocabulary were we committed to this position.

It is perhaps proper that Hamlet had recourse to this concept of truth when he staged a mild insanity to deceive false friends, and argued, "For there's nothing good or bad but thinking makes it so." One of the world's greatest realists asked the question which is deadly to psychological certainty: "Which of you by taking thought can add one cubit to his stature?" None the less, it has been comfortably preached to us that the very intensity of our desire for something is a valid indication of its possibility, not to say probability. And heaven has done yeoman service at the critical juncture of actualization — for if one cannot get his heart's fondest desire here, he will enjoy it hereafter.

In opposition to this type of thought logical certainty measures the truth of a proposition by examining its relationship to an accepted body of truth.[5] A true proposition is one

---

[5] I am postponing to a later chapter consideration of the very important distinction between necessary and contingent propositions, certain and probable truths.

which is related to such a body by the laws of strict inference. This mode of thought has a noble history. Philosophy, theology and science have used it. Although, as we
saw in an earlier chapter, they proceed by different criteria
of truth, they are at one in their aim to construct an impres-
sive system of accepted principles, doctrines or laws by which
to determine the validity of hypothetical or theoretical propositions. Platonic and Aristotelian philosophies constituted
systems in which art, ethics and politics were mutually sustaining parts of an organic whole. Consequently a new
theory in any of these fields was examined not alone in terms
of the particular one it aimed to displace but also as to re-
percussions in the system as a whole. The august theologies
of Origen and Aquinas, as well as Newtonian physics, are
similar in logical structure and practical intent to such philosophical systems.

This is an almost inevitable development. No proposition
stands alone. Its truth value grows in proportion to its ability to gather around itself other and relevant propositions.
Logical certainty derives from the allocation of a principle,
belief or theory in a system of principles, beliefs or theories
which is not questioned and which sustains mutually implicative relations with the newcomer. Mathematical or deductive reasoning is the usual prototype for such system
building, because in it we have our clearest picture of logical validity. In it the entire movement of thought is from
axioms, self-evident truths, and postulates to conclusions
which can be demonstrated to be valid inferences.

But it is now commonplace that neither philosophy, theology nor science has been able fully to introduce mathematical reasoning into its various problems. And this for
the simple reason that they have not been able to construct

fixed and permanently acceptable bodies of truths against which to measure the validity of new theories. Such accumulations of truths are always answerable to experience and therefore are liable to modification if not to dismantling. When a new idea is declared false because it does not fit into established patterns it need not accept this judgment as final. But in order to get a hearing it must gather around itself a growing body of truths which as a system is able to demonstrate its superiority to the system which rejected it.

For example, the revolutionary conception of Copernicus, namely, that we live in a heliocentric universe, was first advanced by Aristarchus of Samos, who lived about 270 b.c. Why was it rejected then, yet accepted almost two thousand years later? It was rejected because it ran counter to all the accepted truths of that day. Aristarchus barely escaped indictment for impiety. Hipparchus and Ptolemy frowned upon the theory and advanced the geocentric view. Aristarchus' theory stood almost alone. It was based upon some acute observations, but they were few in number and fragmentary in character. Almost the same hypothesis was advanced by Copernicus with the significant difference that he had bolstered it by some ancillary theories as to the character of the orbits of heavenly bodies and these in turn rested upon observations and careful calculations. Tycho Brahe and Kepler took up Copernicus' work which ran counter to the prevailing Ptolemaic system and further entrenched it by more accurate observations and calculations. The upshot of their collective work was a formidable system which was able to make good its challenge to a system that had been accepted as the body of truth for over two thousand years.

Thus it is for a new insight in any area. It gets a hearing only when it is found to be relevant to the accepted body of truth or, failing that, when it organizes around itself another system. Whereas psychological certainty locates truth in the emotional intensity which an insight or belief evokes, logical certainty pronounces it true when it has been integrated in an accepted body of truth.

CERTAINTY OF CONCLUSION AND CERTAINTY OF METHOD

Certainty of conclusion and certainty of method are more clearly separated from each other than they are from the two types discussed in the preceding pages. The justification for special attention is that each one of the four types denotes some particular aspect of the problem.

The distinguishing characteristic of certainty of conclusion is that it simply affirms some particular relationship between man and his world.[6] It does not argue the advisability of the choice; it demands its adoption. The method by which the conclusion is reached receives scant attention and questions regarding it are not welcomed, but the indubitable truth of the conclusion is affirmed and loyalty to it required.

One quickly perceives that this type of certainty depends for its significance upon complete acceptance of authority of some kind or other. The morality of primitive and relatively isolated groups is of this nature. For a thousand years or more the Roman Catholic Church swayed Europe because Europe had confidence in the conclusions which the church pressed upon it. In so far as there is a cult of science among us, composed of those who blindly worship the scientist and his work, the emphasis falls upon certainty of conclusion.

[6] W. A. Brown, *Pathways to Certainty* (New York: Charles Scribner's Sons, 1930), p. 23: "Certainty is certainty of something — a truth to be believed or a reality to be experienced."

While we are impressed by the grandeur of the conclusions based upon authority, two closely related questions arise and demand an answer. One wants to know whether we really know enough about the world to speak with such consuming certainty about its fundamental characteristics. The margin of mystery which clusters around the grandiose assertion of many philosophers, theologians and scientists is too narrow to be convincing. However, there is always a remote possibility that the assertions are really true, although the history of thought does not encourage that belief. Briefly, may we not ask the producer of conclusions to withhold his peremptory demand for our acceptance *until* he has stated and successfully defended his theory of knowledge? Whoever urges acceptance of conclusions "because they're so" almost certainly is trying to evade the troublesome problems of knowledge which continue to perplex modern philosophy. This fact definitely pushes the entire problem out of the area of conclusions and into that of method. Thereafter the quest becomes a search for that method of thought which is best fitted to discover and sustain a reliable relationship between man and his world.

When two conclusions are in conflict their exponents must endeavor to demonstrate their validity by explaining the process by which they have been reached. This demands that the evidence and the logic which underlie the conclusions be brought to light. It is perhaps significant in this connection that discoveries in science are never boldly announced as conclusions but are always presented together with an exact description of the procedure by which they were made. Specialists in the field concerned labor carefully over every detail in the method in order to determine the validity of the conclusion. Something akin to this occurs whenever conflict in conclusions is encountered. Therefore we must now focus attention upon the various methods by which men have tried to win certainty.

The one which most readily comes to mind is acceptance of authority, whether it be that of a church, a book, a man, a philosophic system or a scientific world view. This is a very popular way of gaining certainty, and so long as there is neither conflict with other conclusions nor penetrating criticism of the ones proffered, authority rides the crest of the wave. But it is practically impossible to keep authority in this state of supremacy. Some event or person is always demanding the reason back of the conclusions. Only un-reasoning dogmatism can refuse to admit the justice of the request. So our immediate problem is to discover and con-sider the basic categories within whose bosom the various authorities finally seek refuge.

One of the most important of these is intuitionism, which may be defined as the supra-rational perception of truths. Supra-rationalism is its distinguishing token, indicating that its discoveries are independent of logical reflective processes. Intuitionism does not claim that its truths are contra-rational; in fact it is more than likely to claim that they are amenable to the tools of reason *after* they have been laid bare by the moment of supra-rational insight. The fact of discovery is not due to rational processes, though the truths discovered may lend themselves to rational interpretation and system-atization.

A further characteristic of intuitionism as a means to knowledge is indicated by the concept " supra-rational," namely, that the data upon which it proceeds are not sen-sory in character. As we shall presently see, the successful mystic is one who can lay aside the data of normal experience and ascend toward the vision of God; one of the favorite descriptions of the process is "the flight of the Alone to the Alone." Here again we must not infer that the discoveries made in the area of supra-sensory experience are by definition hostile or unrelatable to mundane experiences. Rather the consensus of opinion among Christian mystics, at least, is that these ecstatic experiences make possible an *evaluation* of commonplace experiences in terms of the truths discovered in the moment of union with God.

When we grasp the fact that intuitionism dispenses with logical processes and sensory data in its apprehension of truth, we are prepared for the conclusion that its truths exhibit the character of revelations, of full-fledged creations which spring from the yawning mystery of the universe and invade the passive soul of the mystic. Although this phraseology best fits religious mystics, its basic principle, namely, that intuition is the perception of revelation, is widely applicable.

Nicolai Hartmann, who is skeptically tolerant of religion, asserts that man has an intuitional consciousness by means of which he discerns the realm of values in all its transcendent splendor.[7] George Santayana, to whom religion is a form of poignant art, asserts that man has an "intuition of essence" which is the sole foundation of knowledge — all else is animal faith.[8]

It is difficult to make a brief critique of so important an avenue to certainty, but its strength and weakness can be indicated. The strength of intuitionism lies in the fact that it is an operative factor in any and every discovery, since in the moment of discovery there is a reaching out beyond

---

[7] *Ethics* (New York: The Macmillan Co., 1932), I, chap. 6.
[8] *Skepticism and Animal Faith* (New York: Charles Scribner's Sons, 1923).

observed data to a perception of a more inclusive arrangement or explanation of them.[9] Generalizations or hypotheses are basically adventures in intuition, attempts to grasp something not given yet relevant to the data under consideration. Precisely the same principle is implicit in Sir Isaac Newton's discovery of the law of gravitation and in St. Paul's perception of the all-sufficiency of Jesus Christ. There is a significant difference in the area of verifiability, since the logical method and experimental evidences were much more conclusively marshaled to support Newton's generalization than may ever be possible for St. Paul's adventurous affirmation. These two examples are put in juxtaposition in order to show the scope, hence the strength, of the method of intuitionism.

Its weakness is palpable and is generally recognized. In the first place, its truths are beyond correction or need of it if the supra-rational character of their discovery is emphasized. Within the area of science this failing does not often occur because evidence and logic quickly make the insights useless or confirm them. Religious mysticism has always been dogged by the specter of discrepancies. If a discrepancy occurs between two intuitionists' versions of their experience of God, either it must remain a discrepancy or be attributed to the waywardness of language. This latter exit has been used with appalling frequency.

A second weakness — and once more it is most obvious in the domain of philosophy and religion — is the tendency of religious mysticism to assume a type of metaphysical dualism, the reality of which can be proved only by a recourse to intuition. It professes to describe existence as it is for any

[9] Cf. George Thomas' paper, " A Reasoned Faith," in *The Nature of Religious Experience,* J. S. Bixler, ed. (New York: Harper & Bros., 1937), p. 64.

and all on the basis of evidence gathered by an ultimately esoteric method. By metaphysical dualism I mean two areas of truth, one encountered in sense data, the other mediated by supra-sensuous revelations. This picture of the stratification of reality may be an accurate one, but the weakness of intuitionism lies in the fact that there is no way whereby two intuitionists can confirm each other's testimony to the nature of truth by revelation. I am not raising this as an insuperable obstacle to intuitionism, but it does indicate the area in which the method encounters most of its opposition as the pathway to certainty.

There is another method by which certainty may be won and it impresses me as being the most promising we have. I refer to the method of observation and reason. Not as evidence of its validity but rather as testimonial to its significance, we may note the fact that John Dewey, an empiricist, and Morris Cohen, a rationalist, both pronounce their blessings upon it. Dewey becomes almost reverent in his description of it: " There are a steadily increasing number of persons who find security in methods of inquiry, of observation, experiment, of forming and following working hypotheses. Such persons are not unsettled by the upsetting of any special belief, because they retain security of procedure. They can say, borrowing language from another context, though this method slay my most cherished beliefs, yet will I trust it! " [10]

More precisely, there are three reasons why this method is best fitted to aid us in our quest for truth. First, it is true to the nature of reflective thought. Second, it is self-corrective. Third, it permits adequate communication. An amplification of each of these reasons, together with a con-

[10] *Characters and Events*, II, 437.

sideration of the prime objection, will yield a comprehensive survey of both the strength and the weakness of this method.

1. The method of observation and reason is true to the nature of reflective thought. Thought operates between two poles: the interested organism (not mind alone) and an objective world. The problem of all life can be stated in terms of adjustment of organism to environment so as to sustain and promote life. Ultimately, for all forms of life, the search for this rapport proceeds by trial and error — " The best laid schemes o' mice an' men gang aft a-gley." Reflective thought, as distinct from more passive types of mental activity, occurs when the even flow of attention strikes a snag. It is basically problem solving, as Dewey points out in *How We Think*. One of the characteristics which distinguish man from other forms of life is the way he can react in moments of frustration. Instead of frantically surging this way and that, blindly searching for a solution by fair means or foul, man is capable of a " delayed response," that is, he can pause before the problem and consider various possible solutions.

It is impossible to improve upon the clarity of Professor Edwin A. Burtt's analysis of the five steps involved in reflective thought: (1) occurrence of something felt as a perplexity; (2) observation, designed to make clear precisely what the difficulty is; (3) occurrence to the mind of suggested solutions of the difficulty; (4) reasoning out the consequences involved in the suggestions thus entertained, and evaluating the suggestions by their aid; (5) observation or experiment to test by empirical fact the suggested solutions in the light of their implications.[11]

---

[11] *Principles and Problems of Right Thinking* (revised ed., New York: Harper & Bros., 1931), chap. 4, *passim*.

If this is an adequate description of reflective thought, it is apparent that the method of observation and reason is as old as man's capacity for reflection, and represents the highest development of a method of adjustment which is as old as life itself.

But objections are forthcoming. John Oman,[12] William Temple [13] and F. R. Tennant,[14] eminent English philosophers of religion, unite in pointing out that this method is too narrow to provide in and of itself an adequate approach to reality. It does yeoman service so long as the problem under consideration is in a carefully circumscribed area, but when one endeavors to probe to the depths of reality with it, its inadequacy is readily manifest. Its weakness can be stated in simple terms: Observations are limited by hypotheses and reason conforms to past experience. If the problem is to identify a historical specimen, these limitations will not prove serious. But what if the problem is whether there is cosmic purpose? What then would you observe? How would you formulate hypotheses? Is not reason in need of faith when approaching this vast problem?

Although no conclusive answer to such questions is forthcoming, an approach to an answer is suggested by the second reason which I would offer for the acceptance of this method.

2. *It is self-corrective*. Morris Cohen [15] emphasizes this as its unique characteristic. It alone among methods of thought candidly recognizes the weakness which inheres in its procedure and the margin of error in its conclusions. But recognition of these failings is the first phase of a twofold reaction,

---

[12] *Natural and Supernatural.*

[13] *Christianity in Thought and Practice* (New York: Morehouse Publishing Co., 1936).

[14] *Philosophy of the Sciences* (London: Cambridge University Press, 1932).

[15] *Op. cit.,* p. 155.

the second phase of which is the endeavor systematically to overcome them.

Consider the general objection to the adequacy of the method — the argument that observation proceeds by means of definite hypotheses which act as blinders on the eyes of the observer. Whoever feels that a given hypothesis is too narrow is invited, nay, urged, to submit another not susceptible to this fault. The history of thought is one long testimony to the fact that new hypotheses issue in the discovery of new truths. Let it be admitted that the method of observation and reason will never, by one grand coup, force reality as a whole to capitulate to human knowledge. It proceeds step by step, first in this sector, then in that, pushing steadily at the front line of ignorance of reality. Whoever criticizes it, aids it. That it, at best, yields a piecemeal knowledge of reality is true. It would be a miserable method indeed if we possessed a reliable way of grasping reality in its entirety or in some essence. Various theories of knowledge purport to give this desideratum but not one is able to command a significant following. All such finally revolve into special brands of intuitionism and we have just seen how unreliable this method is.

Lacking, then, a method for laying firm hands on things as a whole, we have little choice but to proceed by the method which can deal convincingly with aspects of the whole. We need not thereby give up as valueless the notion of the whole because, as we have seen, science is producing ever enlarging bodies of knowledge in various areas. Philosophy in its speculative and synthetic moods is endeavoring to discover principles common and fundamental to all. The birth of several metaphysical schemes (those of Whitehead, S. Alexander, Boodin *et al.*) testifies to the possibilities of success. Then, too, theology's new lease on life derives from the fact that creative minds are endeavoring to relate the known problems of human need to the knowledge we have of the universe. Widely divergent systems testify both to the virility of the enterprise and to the inconclusive character of metaphysical thought. There can be no important theology without a convincing philosophy, and this because philosophy endeavors to systematize our knowledge of the world, whereas theology attempts to relate such philosophical first principles to human needs.

If the preceding analysis is accurate, observation and reason are the method which underlies significant development in science, philosophy and theology. The corpus of scientific knowledge, as well as philosophical and theological formulations, grows by steady adherence to it. It is not above reproach, but it is more so than any other method, not alone because it is self-corrective but also because it possesses another and a unique virtue.

3. *It permits communication both as to procedure and as to conclusions.* In no other regard is it in more vivid contrast with intuitionism. Intuitionism as the supra-rational awareness or apprehension of reality simply cannot transmit this experience by means of the social symbolism called language. Thoroughgoing intuitionists have been quick to recognize this failing. Plato laments the fact that the daring soul who left the cave to gaze on the sun stumbled as he returned to its gloom and endeavored to tell its jeering occupants what he had seen. St. John of the Cross is true to the entire tradition of Christian mysticism when he frankly acknowledges that he has no means of conveying to others the import of his visions and ecstasies. The intuitionist may turn to the various arts and charge their symbols with his message, and when he has done this his attempts at communication are at an end.

He has no way of knowing whether he has conveyed even a portion of his experience to the outsider. The matter might be summed up thus: Intuitionism apparently yields a rich harvest of knowledge to the individual intuitionist, but he must play the miser with it, though through no fault of his own. Observation and reason yield knowledge which all intuitionists agree in dubbing " barren," " meager," " sterile," " scrappy," or " integrated nonsense." But this method possesses the important advantage of having a public character by which all who seek may learn. The pathway to testing lies open to any and all who care to travel it.

At the opening of the chapter it was suggested that certainty be defined as man's consciousness of a reliable relationship, stated in terms of beliefs, between himself and his world. The method of observation and reason provides the only certainly *reliable* relationship, because it is the only method of relating man to his world that makes a place for the uneliminable margin of ignorance and error which borders human knowledge and sets out systematically to reduce it as far as possible.

To accept this statement does not mean that the other types of certainty are useless. On the contrary, they are gathered by it into an organic whole where they comprise indispensable aspects of it. There is a necessary and inevitable amount of psychological certainty in the feeling that this method is valid and applicable. Lacking conclusive proof, we accept and follow this method as the best lead we have. Likewise, logical certainty is part and parcel of the method because the prime purpose of observation and reason is to produce an integrated body of beliefs, mutually implicative and sustaining. Obviously the method has merit only because it promises to yield conclusions which are truer than those delivered by any other method, hence certainty of conclusion is admitted as a legitimate member of the household. But I cannot too vigorously insist that emphasis must not fall upon a feeling, or a system, or a conclusion; it must rest squarely upon the method by which these are examined and by which their validity is tested.

Religion can well afford to investigate the meaning of this method for its peculiar province — the relating of life to God, the value structure of the universe. We have seen how man through the ages has groped toward a reliable relationship in this area. A widening circle of thinkers in religion is convinced that the method just described, by making the desired relationship more accurately articulate, will heighten the initial sense of security which roots in the consciousness of value.

Yet we must frankly admit that on the whole philosophies of religion will look askance at this interpretation of the meaning of certainty. To them, the method suggested will doubtless constitute another example of throwing out the baby with the bath. I am convinced that their reluctance to use the method of observation and reason as the guide in the quest for religious certainty is attributable not so much to supreme confidence in other methods as to a misunderstanding of the tentative and incomplete nature of the conclusions which it yields. This misunderstanding is so deep-seated and widespread that it must be dealt with at this point. If, through the next four chapters, the probing seems overcautious, it would be well to remember that the source of infection lies deep and close to the very heart of religious thought.

IV

THE MEANING OF TENTATIVENESS

DEFENDERS of philosophies of religion based upon either authoritarianism or intuitionism will be quick to object that the method of observation and reason does not lead to indubitable conclusions. At most, they reason, it can only claim that the conclusions proffered are the best available and that it is endeavoring to make them truer approximations of reality. The conclusions, then, are not absolute and must be held subject to further investigation — that is, tentatively. Now it is argued that a tentative conclusion is entirely appropriate in the market places and laboratories of life but that it has no place in religion. Professors Wilhelm Pauck and William Adams Brown represent the majority of theologians when they claim that tentativeness means the death of religion.[1] The secret of religious power is commitment to concrete objectives as well as to the generalized ideal (Kingdom of God); science proceeds by objectivity and disinterestedness. Tentativeness is the breath of life to science but a blight upon the vitality of religion. Introduce tentativeness into religion, these writers say, and its reality and power will disappear like a morning mist at sunrise.

The conclusions advanced by observation and reason in any area, whether in physics or in human values, must be held tentatively. This much of the preceding criticism not only must be acknowledged, but I am prepared to insist upon it.

[1] Pauck, *Karl Barth*, p. 6; W. A. Brown, *Pathways to Certainty*, pp. 210–11 (footnote).

And this because I am convinced that when the notion of tentativeness is carefully and properly handled it is light and vigor rather than darkness and weakness for religion. The contemporary pell-mell flight from tentativeness has given rise to some exaggerated notions of the exact nature of the foe. The thesis I would defend implies the possibility that what we fear in ignorance may when illuminated prove to be our ally.

But the notion of tentativeness in religion is distressing to others besides theologians and ministers. The reaction of these professional religionists is symbolic of a much graver problem. They mirror the quandary in which common folk find themselves when the necessity of modifying traditional religion is forced upon them. Therefore a defense of the place of tentativeness in religion must be stated in terms which will be either understood by or interpretable to those who live by their religion as well as those who also reflect upon it. If the notion of tentativeness served only to arouse drowsy theologians from comfortable slumbers or to distract their attention from curious types of metaphysical calculus, most of us would bid it Godspeed. But when it enters into those areas of life where heads and hearts are weary with toil and doubt, where aching souls, already strained to the breaking point, seek succor of religion — if it enters here unannounced and uninterpreted it will be an unwelcome visitor and may cause untold damage.

We might as well frankly face the fact that possibly no amount of interpretation and explanation can make tentativeness at home in religious living. Only actual experience can do so. But that it is, in vague forms to be sure, at this very moment disrupting the thought and life of a growing number of religious people can hardly be doubted. How else can we explain the avid search for certainty which ministers, theologians and laymen are conducting?

James Gordon Gilkey writes on *The Certainty of God* and declares that his purpose is "to help ordinary men and women find answers to the questions which arise repeatedly in everyday life." [2] William Adams Brown shares this desire in his *Pathways to Certainty* and addresses himself "to the problem of certainty in the simple and direct form in which it meets the men and women of our day who, in the conflicts of contemporary thought, are trying to find some firm foundation for a faith in themselves, in the world, and in God." [3]

This is not the place for a critique of these and similar works that, if we may judge by their closing chapters, feel obligated to reaffirm all the traditional conclusions that have been important in religious thought and life.[4] It seems to me that their exposition and defense of certainty is vitiated by their refusal fairly and adequately to analyze the concept of tentativeness and relate it to their conclusions. What the resulting conclusions might lack in grandiose sweep they would more than retrieve in intellectual integrity.

Perhaps the importance of studying the meaning of tentativeness can be illustrated by the plight in which most of us find our religious faith. We want to be certain enough to live effectively, yet we do not want this certainty to grow into a shell of dogmatism which, while it protects us, deprives us of further growth. Somewhere in one's faith there must be a growing edge if it is to keep pace with and be able to interpret and evaluate one's enlarging experiences. Hard and fast conclusions as to the ultimate nature of things are comfortable —

[2] *Op. cit.* (New York: The Macmillan Co., 1928), p. 7.

[3] *Op. cit.,* pp. x–xi.

[4] Bishop F. J. McConnell's *Religious Certainty* (New York: Methodist Book Concern, 1910) is an honorable exception in this regard.

but only so long as one's experience is relatively static. In my opinion the conception of tentativeness reinforces the sense of certainty, when certainty is defined as a reliable method of relating man to his world. The ensuing discussion, involved though it must necessarily be at times, is an endeavor to state why this is true. Let us first consider certain mistaken conceptions of the meaning of tentativeness.

TWO MISCONCEPTIONS OF TENTATIVENESS

1. Tentativeness is open-mindedness. This is a prevalent misconception and can persist only so long as the terms involved are carelessly handled. Open-mindedness can be so construed as to mean tentativeness, but this is not the ordinary use of the term. Its regular usage gives to it the character of *willingness* to reconsider one's position, to receive new information, to reformulate ideas. One characterized by these attitudes is correctly described as open-minded. But — and this is the crucial point — open-mindedness may or may not characterize any given person. It is descriptive of an act of will. One can be open-minded or not as he chooses. It is a volitional attitude. And a good many factors condition this willingness to do something or other at any given moment. For example, open-mindedness regarding the doctrine of immortality may be the result of any one of a number of events: a good meal, a pleasant journey, a genial companion whose ideas are different from ours, or a sense of social insecurity due to the fact that we are in the company of strangers whose opinions on the subject we do not know. The point I am making is that open-mindedness, as volitional act, may depend upon factors which are not even indirectly related to the truth or falsity of the position about which one suddenly becomes open-minded.

In contrast, tentativeness may roughly be defined as *enforced* open-mindedness. It is not due to volitional caprice occasioned by chance influences which may touch us in some way; it derives from factors directly related to the positions or ideas which are up for consideration. The factors which underlie tentativeness, which make open-mindedness inevitable, can be neither strengthened nor modified by gustatory delight, charming or strange environment. They are, in short, vital facts about the matters under consideration and cannot be tempered or tampered with by extraneous influences. Whereas open-mindedness is optional, that is, conditioned by factors which may be irrelevant to the prime issue, and has therefore only a chameleonlike stability, tentativeness is obligatory, since it derives from factors which are as real as the idea at issue and are indisputably relevant to it.

2. *Tentativeness is acquiescence in confusion.* We rightly associate tentativeness with a condition of confusion, but it is a misconception to associate it with *acquiescence* in such confusion. Tentativeness does not belong to a situation wherein desires are satisfied by maintenance of existing habits. It belongs to a situation where the purposive drive of the organism, the desire-satisfaction cycle, is broken by failure to achieve satisfaction. At that point reflective thought comes into play in order to canvass the various possible ways of reestablishing the flow of purposiveness. Seldom can thought produce an either-or alternative in a concrete case. Multiple possibilities usually are discerned and indicated.

It is precisely in this situation, when the thwarted organism is confronted by a variety of possible solutions, that some persons find the deepest meaning of tentativeness. It denotes someone who is "halted between two opinions" like King Claudius in *Hamlet,* who desires both peace of soul and the very thing which precludes this, namely, continuing in the possession of power. The proverbial mule starving to death between two equally large and tempting stacks of hay is an adequate symbol of this interpretation of tentativeness. It develops its case by arguing that the moment activity is essayed along the line of any one of the alternatives, tentativeness gives way to decision.[5]

I venture to suggest that this conception of tentativeness is too limited. By this I mean to call attention to the fact that tentativeness is an integral part of a larger method used with more or less exactitude in every concrete problem, namely, the method of science. Professor E. A. Burtt points out this larger context when he describes the threefold ideal of science as (1) discovery of universal law, (2) tentativeness in thinking, and (3) exactitude in evaluating results.[6] Apropos tentativeness he writes: "The human achievement which this word represents is really a stupendous one."[7]

The precise point of the larger setting of tentativeness is that it is characteristic of reflective thought whenever, wherever and as long as reflection persists. It is not a state of indecision which one steps out of when he accepts one of several alternatives, unless this alternative restores the organic equilibrium which the conflict disturbed. When we say that tentativeness is coextensive with reflective thought, whether in some exact laboratory enterprise or in some less specialized area, we are giving it a much broader scope than that of the restricted identification as the moment of confusion. It is equally characteristic of the movement away from confusion and is descriptive of the reflective process which persists until

---

[5] Dr. E. S. Ames has called such decision by action a "practical absolute."
[6] *Religion in an Age of Science* (New York: Frederick Stokes & Co., 1929).
[7] *Ibid.*, p. 74.

the harmonious flow of the desire-satisfaction cycle has been re-established. It is not acquiescence in confusion; rather its first step is to acknowledge the reality of confusion, and it then continues as an integral factor in the method by which the confusion is overcome.

FACTORS UNDERLYING TENTATIVENESS

Tentativeness derives from certain logical and cosmological considerations. It rests upon both a characteristic of empirical knowledge and an attribute of empirical metaphysics. Few emphases are more instructive of the uniqueness of contemporary philosophical thought than the widespread attention given to problems of probability in logic and contingency in metaphysics. If probability and contingency are accepted as valid categories (and an increasing number of influential thinkers are so accepting them), then the meanings of tentativeness are here to stay, not in philosophy alone but in religion and in every other attempt to describe the world in general and to evaluate and order human life. Hence scientific, philosophical and religious knowledge are all affected by these two considerations which underlie tentativeness.

1. Empirical truths are probable only. Bishop Butler's famous assertion, " Probability is the very guide of life," is drawn from the matrix of human experience. Only a moment's reflection is necessary to reveal the fact that most of our so-called " certainties " are in reality probabilities. We say with certainty that the sun will rise tomorrow, but second thought always takes the absoluteness from the proposition and steps its certainty down to probability. All this is widely recognized. Professor C. I. Lewis sums it up in a single trenchant sentence: " I would point out, that granting all the universal truth and all the certainty that the most ambitious theory has ever claimed, if it were not for the more lowly knowledge of probabilities based on generalities which have their known exceptions, we would most of us be dead within the week." [8]

In so far as religion retains its empirical note (*This do* and *thou shalt live*), its recommendations must be regarded as probable only. Yet to many there is something heinous in such a position. Even Francis Bacon, who must be given a place of honor among tough-minded thinkers, concluded that "behind spiritual uncertainty lies moral decay." If one wants to cite great men in the Christian tradition one gets even stronger testimonial to the fact that the truths of religion are, or must be regarded as, more than probable. Paul, Origen, Augustine, Aquinas — and almost every other dominant mind — can be drawn as witnesses to this assertion. Though their illuminating insights continue to this day as stars by which we fix our course, we dare not overlook the fact that many of their endeavors to solve specific problems impress us as being something less than profound — witness Paul's advice as to ornaments, veils, hair, place of women in church; the aged Augustine's efforts to determine purity in women.

If someone protests that these objections deal with the minutiae of religion rather than with its broad truths, I can only reply that in so far as they demonstrate the inability of the so-called "broad or fundamental" truths to give infallible guidance in specific problems, such truths are probable only and argue for the reality of the fact of tentativeness in religion and demand its overt recognition.

But what precisely is involved when we say that an empiri-

[8] *Mind and the World Order* (New York: Charles Scribner's Sons, 1929), p. 334.

cal truth is probable only? How much foundation is there for the fear that if all we have is probable truths we cannot defend ourselves and our faith from skepticism? The chapter that follows endeavors to answer these problems by analyzing the nature of probability. Just now we must be content to notice that probability is one of the factors which underlie the notion of tentativeness.

2. *Contingency is characteristic of reality.* As we shall be using the term, "contingency" is synonymous with chance, indeterminacy and unpredictability. It was formerly a member in good standing in the metaphysical fraternity, in fact if not in name. For example, the crux of Plato's speculations is the conception of ideas, or essences, struggling to bring order, form and being into cloddy, inert, intractable matter. But this cosmic thrust is never completely successful. The resultant item always shows its dual parentage. The idea incarnate in matter is always thwarted, degraded, and is forever yearning to be released from its material prison. It is never quite clear in Plato's thought why matter should be so recalcitrant, but the facts of experience seem eloquently and unanimously to affirm that it is so.

Aristotle, using a different pattern of thought — that of biology — made no significant alteration in the basic Platonic conception. For him, the notion of entelechy is that of a form struggling to realize itself through insentient, inert matter, which manages always in some measure to frustrate the effort. Witness the fact that we never see the potential oak in an acorn. What we view is the potential oak as it has fought its way into actuality conditioned by fertility of soil, amount of rainfall and severity of weather.

Then, historically, with the dawn of the age of absolutes — idealistic and otherwise — the doctrine of contingency was thrust out of the philosophical fraternity. This exclusion made it possible for philosophers to slumber quietly on the bosom of the notion of universal law of one sort or another. Newtonian physics provided the sleeping powders which prolonged the slumbers when restiveness was manifested a couple of centuries ago. But at the turn of this century, and for exactly those reasons which led to the devaluation of science,[9] the doctrine returned and created such a commotion that science and philosophy alike have readmitted it, albeit warily, into the circle of the brethren.

Obviously this talk of chance, waywardness, unpredictability as a fundamental characteristic of the universal structure of things must sound perilously like nonsense to the Christian whose doctrine of God has always meant cause, design, order and purpose in things as a whole. His first reaction will probably be to ascribe the entire notion to human ignorance, reasoning that what we call chance is simply an unexplored area in the universe.[10]

How much truth is there in this tendency to equate contingency with human ignorance? Is it possible either logically or actually to conceive of a world in which contingency is an ineradicable factor? In any event, what becomes of the theistic conception of a controlling purpose? These and related questions cannot be answered until we have taken care to see precisely what is involved in the concept of contingency, a venture which will occupy Chapter VI.

[9] Cf. Chap. II.
[10] This is the orthodox Roman Catholic position. Cf. A. D. Sertillanges, *Foundations of Thomistic Philosophy* (London: Sands & Co., 1932). In substantial agreement is H. H. Farmer, *op. cit.,* chap. 6.

THE PRINCIPLE OF POLARITY

The ensuing efforts further to delineate the nature of probability and contingency will make constant use of the principle of polarity as described and defended by Morris Cohen.[11] Therefore a word of explanation about it is now in order.

It is, primarily, a suggestive attempt to provide a method by which the wealth of reality will be treated fairly. As such it is a thoroughgoing protest against the facile attempt to impale reality on the horns of the either-or dilemma. So-called contradictory concepts upon careful examination turn out to be supplementary, so much so that one without the other is lost. Neither alone is true. The truth of the matter lies between them, though there are difficulties in a clear statement of it. In addition, the principle of polarity is definitely opposed to any endeavor to blur or gloss over the differences which inhere in the contradictory concepts. It jealously insists that each one has hold of a vital area of fact and that the total conception will be enriched by the retention of both. Therefore the principle of polarity is aimed not so much at the resolution of contradictions as it is toward the preservation of differences by holding the contradictory concepts together in the belief that the truth lies between them, i.e., in their relationship.

An example would be the venerable philosophical antithesis between individuality and universality. One pauses before using it, since it has been the cause of so much bad blood for two thousand years. Each of the concepts purports adequately to explain reality. Exponents of individuality point out that individuals are all we ever experience whether directly or inferentially. As one of Plato's critics put it,

---

[11] *Reason and Nature*, pp. xi, 18 f., 135.

"Horses I see, but 'horseness' I do not see." But the defenders of universality proceed to show how the so-called individuals are simply manifestations of an enduring substratum from which they derive their distinguishing characteristics. Hence the locus of reality is in the substratum rather than in its temporary manifestation. Plato would reply to his critic: "When you say you see horses, what you mean, among other things, is that you behold something which is familiar, that is, it exhibits the characteristics common to 'horse' rather than fowl. If you say you see a brown horse, the color is universal in precisely the same sense as horse is. Therefore any individual horse is ultimately a temporary pattern of universals." The principle of polarity is an honest endeavor to hold the truths of both contestants together because reality answers to both descriptions despite their contradictory aspects.

We shall have cause to see that probability and certainty as well as contingency and structure demand the rigorous use of this principle of interpretation. But we must guard against that facile use of it by which one foregoes all effort to resolve the contradiction. Herein lies the genius of science and scientific method. It is a ceaseless endeavor to resolve the differences by discovering a system of meanings inclusive of them. We shall see concrete cases of how this works in the following chapters on probability and contingency.

V

THE NATURE OF PROBABILITY

IF WE ARE to capture the meaning of this elusive concept, probability, we must move both comprehensively and patiently. And success demands that we venture into the difficult and oftentimes poorly lighted haunts of the logician. But he has much to teach us on this point since the problem of probability is, as we shall see, largely a logical one. It arises in connection with a certain type of judgment which is the stuff of empirical knowledge. However, there is another type of judgment, based upon a priori or rational or necessary truths, in which probability has no place whatsoever. The meaning and importance of the notion of probability cannot be determined until we " spot " probability on the map of logic, so to speak. When we see that it is an integral aspect of all empirical knowledge, and remember that religion has always striven to put its message in terms of such knowledge, we shall be in a position to gauge, in some measure, its impact upon religion. Our first step in this direction is to get a firmer grasp on the two general types of logical judgments; then we shall take a cross section of what is meant by empirical knowledge.

INDUCTIVE AND DEDUCTIVE JUDGMENTS

The Greeks early discerned a significant difference in the properties of the objects which they found in their world. Aristotle spoke of this as the necessary and accidental properties of things. He thereby drew a distinction which has wielded tremendous influence on Western thought. Logic, for him, included two methods of thought, induction and deduction. Induction denotes man's endeavor to discover, describe and relate to a deeper causal sequence the accidental properties in order to determine the essential character of things. It takes the world of fact, that is, the world as we find it, a welter of manifestations, and endeavors to discover behind or within it the structure or form which is essential or necessary to its existence. Plato and Aristotle agree that the essence of an object does not lie on its surface but must be ferreted out. For example, the essential part of an oak is not any one of the discernible characteristics such as root, leaf, or bark, but is the formative principle by virtue of whose dynamic operations these manifestations or accidental properties come into existence. They do not explain it but it does explain them. But our only approach to this essence is by way of its manifestations. We never see the oak form; all we encounter is individual oak trees. Induction, in this case, aims faithfully to enumerate and accurately to describe the sensory impressions yielded by oak trees and, proceeding by way of inference, to lay bare to reason the causative principle or form which alone is explanatory of the dynamic nature of an oak tree. Induction is in search of what Morris Cohen calls " some invariant relation that simulates the invariance of logical or mathematical relations." [1]   C. W. Morris points out a profoundly significant implication of inductive thought: " When induction is pressed toward certainty, it collapses into deduction." [2]   Inductive judgments provide the basis of empirical knowledge, information based upon sensory impressions.

[1] *Reason and Nature*, p. 119.
[2] Unpublished class lectures, University of Chicago, 1933.

At first glance deduction is worlds removed from induction. It proceeds from the essential principle to some concrete embodiment of it. Needless to say, examples drawn from fields other than logic (syllogistic) and mathematics (whose procedure parallels that of syllogistic logic) are not forthcoming. Biology is an inductive rather than a deductive science because it is in search of the invariant principle which explains various manifestations of life.

Inductive judgments take the form of existential propositions; e.g., the book is red, or the tree is fifty feet in height. Such propositions constitute empirical knowledge. They are descriptive of the thousand and one judgments we make in the course of every day relative to clothes, weather, companions, contests, etc. They are equally descriptive of the biological and social sciences which proceed from observation of particulars to formulation of generalizations.

Deductive judgments take the form of tautological propositions. These are harder for laymen in logic to grasp. They are not concerned about existence, the world of concrete objects. They deal with the logical implications of a concept or a system of concepts. Their purpose is to make clearer the precise implications of the premises from which the judgment proceeds. The classic syllogism: "All men are mortal; Socrates is a man; therefore Socrates is mortal," illustrates the point. The conclusion simply calls attention to a specific implication of the premises.

There is a clear illustration of the difference between tautological and existential propositions. The properties of a perfect circle or a perfect lever can be enunciated with a clarity and precision which yield indisputable certainty, not because anyone has ever seen, measured or balanced such, but precisely because the argument proceeds by definition of concepts rather than by manipulation of existential materials. It is one thing to reason: "The area of *a* circle is reached by πr^2," and quite another to infer: "The area of *this* circle is yielded by πr^2." The first proposition is tautological (prescriptive,[3] in that it states what, by definition, must be so); the second is existential (descriptive, in that it states what, after experimentation, may prove to be true).

Induction and deduction being thus pushed so far apart it may seem gratuitous to show wherein they are vitally interdependent. Yet contemporary logicians insist that this must be done. Whitehead somewhere remarks that induction and deduction are two ends of the same worm. Morris Cohen is of the opinion that "induction and deduction are not . . . antithetic terms in the realm of purely formal logic. The difference between them is one concerning material evidence."[4] Exactly how they supplement each other will be apparent, I think, when we have spent some time analyzing the units of empirical knowledge.

ANALYSIS OF EMPIRICAL KNOWLEDGE[5]

Strictly speaking, the simplest possible unit of empirical knowledge has three distinct aspects or phases. These commingle as an organic unity in the flow of conscious processes and are discernible as separate constituents only when we inject the catalyst of logical analysis. The interdependent nature of the constituents makes an exposition of them as separate entities difficult because a satisfactory clarification of one is impossible prior to an introduction and at least partial

[3] The terms "prescriptive" and "descriptive" were suggested by C. W. Morris in unpublished class lectures, 1933.

[4] *Op. cit.,* p. 119.

[5] The outline of this section is suggested by C. I. Lewis, *Mind and the World Order.*

explanation of the other two. But our present task is to locate the source of probability, and since that appears to be somewhere in the area of empirical knowledge we must proceed with the analysis.

The constituents of the unit of empirical knowledge in the order in which they will be discussed are: (1) sense data or the " given "; (2) meanings or the concept; (3) consequences or verification. Understand now, we are dealing with the world of concrete realities which flows by every moment of every day of every sentient organism. The function of thought in the milieu is eminently practical, as we have seen. Knowledge gained in this area is empirical knowledge, and from it stems the nature of probability.

1. Sense Data or the Given. The naïve realist (and this catches most of us) simply takes the witness of his senses at its face value. They carry with them the overtone of objectivity, and he does not demur. He does not see redness, feel roundness and taste sweetness. He sees, feels and eats an apple that is red, round and sweet. For him all qualitative variations are inherent in objects, and are not the product of subjective reactions.

But naïve realism is surrounded by caustic critics who constantly call attention to the facts of illusion and disagreement between two observers of the same objective reality. The debate is characterized by many subtle distinctions which with proper and tender care flower into various theories of knowledge. Although our present purpose does not permit a description of these differences, I would not thereby give the impression that they are unimportant, because the reverse is true so far as philosophy in general is concerned. But for our special purpose we need only note that all schools agree that the mind begins to work with some item or other which is not created *in toto* but which has an independent character of its own. This we shall recognize hereinafter as "the given." Several facets of it demand attention.

a) The given is based upon sensory impressions. (Other synonyms are "qualia," "sensa" or "sense data.") The simple fact about these impressions is that they have objective validity. That is, they are manifestations or aspects of an external reality. This is plain enough when we contend that the sensory impressions provoked by a tree trunk indicate a reality objective to the observer. Yet the principle is precisely the same when the sensa comprising the given spring from dreams or illusions. Such phenomena per se are as objectively real as the tree trunk in that they stimulate conscious behavior. They have to do with things rich in sensory images — things seen, heard, felt. In short, illusions or dreams are things actually experienced, in a queer distorted way, perhaps, but none the less as truly objective for empirical inquiry as any object in the environment outside the organism.[6] What we know, empirically speaking, must come fundamentally through sensory impressions. If, as Oman and the mystics claim, there is knowledge beyond these sense impressions, then the only point I care now to make is that it is not empirical knowledge.

b) The given is incomplete. It is never a revelation of the actual and potential concreteness of the parent object. It is a genuine clue to this fuller nature though, and deserves consideration for this reason. The given is a clue to types of activity which, as we shall see in the next two sections, aim to reveal the more inclusive nature of the object. An object per se is never given in experience. All impressions of it are relative to the perceiver. This does not in any way invalidate

[6] Sigmund Freud, *The Interpretation of Dreams* (New York: The Macmillan Co., 1933).

the fact that the given is a real and reliable perspective of the object; it is, so to speak, the object viewed a certain way. This characteristic of the given adumbrates the conclusion that what we mean by "object" is the objective focal point of varieties of perspectives.

c) The given is singled out, as a rule, by the run of attention of the total organism, yet maintains its objective identity. A botanist bent on discovering and classifying the flowers of a given locality will be sensitive to the visual sensations which are the given of flowers and may totally neglect the animal life which is as real as flowers though not relevant to his pursuit. It can be laid down as a general rule that we see what we look for; that the dominant interest determines what sensa or qualia are actually perceived and become the clue to inductive generalizations and the basis of empirical knowledge.

One form of subjectivism is likely to intrude at this point and therefore deserves special attention. It maintains that we see only what we look for; that experience is wholly at the behest of desire. Anyone who has heard a tornado or hurricane hurtle by knows better. No one desires these, or earthquakes, floods, illness, etc., yet they inject themselves prominently into experience. It is possible to give due weight to the tendency of interest to narrow perception without going to the extreme just mentioned. I venture the opinion that the objective character of the given, which is so obvious in these cases, is descriptive of its nature wherever and whenever perceived. The botanist is willing to accept novelty in a specimen; in fact, contemporary movements in science are recovering considerable humility in the presence of their materials. Surprises are hoped for and welcomed as eagerly as they are avidly catalogued and explained.

d) The given is apprehended by means of concepts. The

botanist is not looking for purely sense data; he is searching for flowers. Granted, his only contact with them is via sensory impressions, yet the concept " flower " denotes a cluster of meanings of which color, odor and structure are specific aspects. The given as sense data is merely candidating for the status of knowledge. It must be conceptualized, placed in an inclusive system of meanings by means of successful predication of consequences, before it becomes empirical knowledge.

2. *Meanings or the Concept*. Here, it seems to me, instrumentalism scores a clean-cut decision over other philosophical schools. For it, meaning is potential doing. To discover the meaning of a specimen, a new word, idea or custom is to secure fuller information as to its environs; that is to say, what its functions are in the light of the totality of which it is a part.[7] Empirical knowledge is funded in concepts which are best understood as clusters of meanings. Another way of stating it is that the concept is a summary of experience and is brought by the mind as a priori truth to the given in any particular case. A traveler in the dusk of evening, expecting trouble, shall we say, receives a set of sensory impressions, visual and auditory, pertaining to something by the roadside. Past experiences, including stories of such happenings, of things " that " shape, of " that " sound, rush forward in the form of concepts and suggest ways of reacting. " It " may be a stump, or an animal or a crouching man, amid swaying bushes. Each possibility is embodied in a concept which suggests appropriate types of reaction. In any event, what the traveler needs is more information about " that." He secures this by selecting the most promising concept, stump, let us say, and

---

[7] Bridgman, *The Logic of Modern Physics*, insists that all scientific concepts are fundamentally " operational."

checking up on it. If "it" is a stump, then he can treat it in certain ways. If he approaches it as a stump and it springs at him, another concept (perhaps another man) is necessary to explain the augmented character of the original given. Empirical knowledge of what any "it" or "that" is an aspect of awaits the application of concepts until the predictions or meanings implicit in one fit the behavior of the objective reality.

George Herbert Mead makes much of the fact that we learn through actual and imaginative manipulation. Every object has a "manipulatory area" and we embody in our concept of that object the various ways we can work with it. Whether our description of it is accurate can be determined only by experience. If we can manipulate it according to prediction, we label that concept true.

Several pointed assertions can be made as to the nature of the concept, so conceived.

a) In the first place, it is a summary of past experience. It is what we have learned to expect in similar situations encountered in the past. Concepts, therefore, grow with experience. Such commonly used ones as matter, energy, life, mind, God are cases in point. They gather into themselves all the findings of all the experiments and reflections conducted within certain areas to date. They are endeavors to predict the fuller nature of any problematic sense data or given on the basis of this aggregate of experience. Another way of stating it is that concepts denote meaningful ways of dealing with any specific given in order to discover the fuller nature of the objective reality which the given mediates to the mind.

b) Another and equally important characteristic is that a concept is always a priori to any particular judgment which utilizes it. A priori, for our purpose, designates the fact that we have past experience summarized in the form of units, conveniently precise. Such units of meaning are called concepts and are accepted truths prior to the problem. Sensory impressions are never simply received; they are objects of more or less immediate reaction, which, in turn, rests on previous experience. We approach a given with a mind teeming with possible interpretations of its fuller significance. Those psychologists who argue that our run of interest determines what we see have exploited this truth.

c) A third aspect of a concept is that when it endeavors to deal with existential data about which empirical evidence is possible, its truth value for empirical evidence must be tested by consequences. William James pointed out that the most important thing about a concept is its " cash value." He further insisted that you could tell words, like trees, by their fruits. Whether past experience adequately interprets a present problem or whether the latter will reveal some latent characteristic and thereby change the concept is not germane to our present purpose. The fundamental point to keep in mind is that the truth of an empirical judgment cannot be determined before the eventuation of the predictions implicit in the concept.

3. Consequences or Verification. All that has been said about the given and the concept can be applied either directly or indirectly to the meaning of consequences. James's " cash value," Mead's " manipulatory area " and Dewey's " instrumentalism " one and all deal with verification through fulfillment of predicated activity. For empirical knowledge, then, the measure of truth inherent in a concept is determined by the accuracy with which it adumbrates the fuller nature of the object to which the given acts as clue. Verification, so conceived, occurs after, not before, the act of applying the meanings which constitute the concept.

As we have seen, the concept endeavors to confer full-blown individuality upon the given. It is a judgment as to the character of the whole of which only a part is given. Verification, therefore, indicates that the meaningful activity implicit in the concept is descriptive of the fuller character of the object. The blur in the bushes by the roadside may be stump or man or lurking beast of prey. Fuller experience alone can tell which is the truer concept. If the traveler flees down the road without gaining further knowledge of the blur, he may be a safer, but most assuredly he will not be a wiser man. His knowledge of the object in the bushes begins and ends with the assertion regarding his visual and auditory impressions of its indistinct shape and inconclusive sound. The only real fact in his knowledge of the whole situation is this: he thought he saw and heard something in the bushes.

EMPIRICAL KNOWLEDGE AND PROBABILITY

We are now ready to spend some time with the notion, mentioned earlier, that induction and deduction are supplementary aspects of empirical knowledge. The quickest way to the heart of the matter is to make, then illustrate and justify, the assertion that logical validity is essential to the growth of empirical truth; that is to say that deduction is operative in the development of inductive knowledge. Or what logicians regard as certain truth is an integral factor in the achievement of probable truth. If this can be shown to be the case, we are then in a position to define and thereby place in usable form the notion of probability.

A dramatic but fair example of how empirical knowledge grows occurred several years ago.[8] Mayor Cermak of Chicago, struck down by an assassin's bullet, hovered between life and death for several days. The doctors, specialists all, disagreed as to his chances of recovery. The morning paper for February 26, 1933, carried the following items that are pertinent to our problem: (1) an electric cardiogram showed that definite damage had been wrought in the mayor's heart structure in the past twelve hours; (2) he was sleeping only under the influence of opiates; (3) his blood pressure, temperature and respiration were no more alarming than they had been the day before. On the basis of these and, of course, other data not published (but presumably the same for all of them) the doctors issued a bulletin which indicated that while the mayor's condition was somewhat worse than it had been, they sharply disagreed as to the outcome. Three felt he had a chance to live; one felt that he was certain to die, and that shortly. The latter added that he might be wrong but didn't think so.

A little reflection shows that these judgments can be placed in the framework of the syllogism (deductive logic):

Major premise: All patients characterized by certain data have more than an even chance to live (or die, said one doctor).

Minor premise: This patient exhibits these data (same for all).

Conclusion: This patient will live (die).

The major premise is an aggregate of each doctor's experience with relevant cases. It constitutes what might be

---

[8] An equally pertinent one is the conflict between the pre-election polls on the presidential campaign of 1936 conducted respectively by Mr. Gallup and the *Literary Digest*.

called a " universe of reference." [9] This can be more carefully described as the group of rationally certified and acceptable propositions which constitute a definite, though usually un-articulated, premise from which the doctor's judgments must proceed. Professor C. I. Lewis writes: " Such ultimate prem-ises . . . must be actual given data for the individual who makes the judgment, hence the probability of a given for-mulation may vary from individual to individual, according to our individual knowledge of a relevant sort." [10]

The minor premise is an item drawn from the flow of ex-perience which is refined by techniques of observation and measurement.

The conclusion, likewise, awaits future events before it be-comes an item of empirical knowledge. Obviously some doctor was wrong on the morning of February 26, 1933; wrong, in that what he predicted would come to pass did not. In this case, the majority was decidedly wrong because Mayor Cermak died within a few days.

Such is the possible fate of all empirical judgments: they may or may not prove true. Only future developments can determine. Hence we sprinkle conclusions of this type with such qualifying words as " likely," " almost certainly," " prob-ably." Obviously, there is a one-to-one ratio between empiri-cal knowledge and probability.

But the point I want to raise now does not permit an easy solution. What is there about empirical judgments which makes them even probably true? Prior to the death of the mayor the conflicting judgments had a measure of probable truth in them. Two factors comprise the major premise

9 J. M. Keynes, *Treatise on Probability* (London: The Macmillan Co., 1921), p. 131.
10 *Op. cit.,* p. 329. Cf. C. D. Broad, " The Relation between Induction and Probability," *Mind* (New Series), XXVII, 391–92.

in these and other empirical judgments, and provide the degree of truth which inheres in the conclusion. They are (1) individual experience of a related sort, and (2) the logical framework by which they are dovetailed into a single comprehensive judgment. Hence when a new and therefore unfinished case is thought to belong to this class the all-inclusive judgment is advanced as a prediction of what to expect. The entire judgmental process is stated in such a way as to be logically valid. The doctor reasons thus: *If* the major premise is true, and *if* the minor premise is true, *then* the conclusion must necessarily follow. Taken as an exercise in deduction, there is no flaw in this reasoning. Even those judgments which proved to be empirically inaccurate were none the less logically valid. Strictly speaking, deductive logic is much more concerned about logical integrity than about the applicability of its conclusions to the existential world.[11] But these doctors were not interested in logical validity. What they were striving for was an accurate prediction of the course of empirical events. We may rest assured that mistake in this famous case not only would repudiate the conclusion but would substantially modify the major premise. Yet the really crucial point for our purpose is that the whole enterprise of empirical truth in this situation depended for growth upon the logical validity of the physicians' reasoning. Not alone conclusion as to eventual outcome, but prescriptions, treatment, etc., were determined by means of the same logical procedure.

Deduction, then, brings to bear in an articulate form past experience of a relevant sort. The case to which it applies its reasoning may not respond as predicted. Only time will

[11] Lewis, *op. cit.*, p. viii: " Logical integrity and concrete applicability are quite separate matters."

tell. But when it does respond it will be used in the construction of a truer universe of reference. Therefore, we see how induction (for the modification or reinforcement of the universe of reference by the case under scrutiny is induction) and deduction are supplementary aspects of empirical procedure.

THE MEANING OF PROBABILITY

Probability characterizes the endeavor of that which is logically valid to become empirically true. This definition describes the precise place in experience where the concept emerges and carries meaning. So to define it is only to summarize the preceding pages of this chapter and to state in succinct form the principle of polarity as it mediates between a priori certainty and empirical probability. When we say that we live by probable rather than by certain truths it is important to keep in mind that without the latter we could never achieve the former.[12] Nothing is more certain than logical validity. Logical inferences are called necessary truths. We have just seen how such inferences are potent factors in the development of empirical truth. An empirical judgment in which logical validity (binding past experience to present problems) is an integral factor is a probable truth. An empirical judgment without logical validity is the wildest form of guesswork.

One of the first reactions to this line of thought can be stated as a question: Is acceptance of probability as the measure of empirical truth tantamount to skepticism? This is important because of the widespread identification of probability and skepticism.

Skepticism derives from what metaphysicians call the possibility of " infinite regress " in an investigation. Archimedes'

[12] *Ibid.*, pp. 310–11.

proud boast that if there were a place to stand he could lift the world with his lever aptly illustrates the meaning of skepticism. There is a place to stand neither for one who wants to lift the world nor for one who wants to do anything else. We are all in Archimedes' predicament — so runs the counsel of skepticism.

It is heartening to laymen to discover that competent logicians regard such reasoning as the common enemy and submerge their differences for the time being to fall upon it with one accord, though from different angles and with different weapons. All insist that probability cannot be equated with skepticism because probability has a place on which to stand, a foothold, a point of departure. The theory of probability as developed by Keynes and Broad derives its nonskeptical character from an assumption as to the " limited variety " [13] in the nature of things. Morris Cohen [14] is in partial agreement with this in his emphasis upon the " assumption of homogeneity " which underlies inductive inference. C. W. Morris is dubious about the inductive hypotheses just mentioned but feels that there is a *method* by which the truth value of a probability can be reached: " The probability of a proposition or argument being true on the next step is, on the simplest version of the frequency theory, the proportion of times the proposition has been true or the argument successful in the past." [15]

Dr. C. I. Lewis, in his *Mind and the World Order,* defends probability against the charge of skepticism by analyzing the basis of David Hume's skepticism regarding causal relation-

[13] Keynes, *op. cit.,* pp. 258 ff.; Broad, *loc. cit.,* XXIX, 42 f.

[14] *Op. cit.,* p. 116.

[15] Unpublished class lectures, 1933. In fairness to Dr. Morris we should not regard this statement as more than a clue to his carefully formulated thought on the meaning of probability.

ships. Hume held that we never see a " cause " or vital inter-relationship. All we see is a series of events. Any kind of connecting link is attributable to our " tendency to feign." Lewis feels that Hume's skepticism must be applied with equal severity to the much more fundamental problem of the recognition of objects. Unless Hume is prepared to be skep-tical about the existence of objects, he has no warrant for be-ing dubious about causal relations among objects. Since Hume accepts the recognition of objects but denies validity to statements as to their interrelations, he is inconsistent. Lewis insists that the principle in both cases is identical.[16] Hence only one who is prepared to lapse into solipsism can be con-sistently skeptical. Lewis constructs his entire theory of knowledge upon the principle involved in the recognition of objects and its extension to the interrelations among them.

Logicians, then, agree that probability is different not in degree but in kind from skepticism. Stated positively, there is some truth value, a definite reliability, in every valid prob-ability. How much, whether measurable — these and other related questions are bitterly disputed.

A probable truth indicates a general direction to be taken rather than a detailed chart of what occupies each foot of the way. Its value derives equally from the comprehensive-ness of past experience of a relevant sort and from the logical integrity of the process by which it is brought to bear upon a particular problem. It is not inerrant. " Probability begins and ends as probability. . . . The importance of probability can only be derived from the judgment that it is *rational* to be guided by it in action; and a practical dependence on it can only be justified by a judgment that in action we *ought* to take some account of it." [17]

[16] *Op. cit.*, p. 354.   [17] Keynes, *op. cit.*, pp. 322 ff.

VI

THE NATURE OF CONTINGENCY

WHEREAS probability is characteristic of empirical knowledge, contingency describes one aspect of empirical reality, i.e., the world disclosed and described by empirical knowledge. It is synonymous with chance, which Professor Spaulding interprets as the "absence of both necessity or impossibility."[1] A tragic and concrete example of this is the act which precipitated the World War. Granted that secret treaty alliances and armament activities had laid a powder train all over Europe, it is none the less a contingent (chance) fact that the assassination of an Austrian archduke was to explode it. The war did not follow this occurrence through any necessity. Any one of a hundred other events might have lighted the holocaust. It is conceivable that this one might have been dealt with, as had many others, so as to avert war. Hence we see that no necessity attaches to the relationship. Neither was this relationship impossible, for, obviously, the war did follow the murder. So when any empirical causal relationship is neither necessary nor impossible, it is contingent in precisely this sense.

But the ancient objection to the notion of contingency must be stated and dealt with. It is to the effect that what we mean by contingency is really human ignorance hyposta-

[1] E. G. Spaulding, *A World of Chance* (New York: The Macmillan Co., 1936), p. vii.

tized and predicated to the universe as a whole. It is argued that contingency is relative to nature as grasped by the human mind, and that it is just possible that, could we but penetrate to her heart, nature is not characterized by chance happenings such as those implied in the notion of objective indeterminism. Whatever truth there is in the notion of contingency can be attributed to human ignorance.

This point of view cannot be dismissed simply because it is usually advanced by persons who want to " tack down all the loose edges of their world." They desire certain causal relationships in all things. They prefer a determinism (the kind, whether spiritual or material, does not matter) to the notion of contingency. Nor does it adequately meet the point to grant that every method we have for approaching nature has its limitations and that, admittedly, these limitations must be reckoned with in every estimate we make of nature. The only nature we shall ever know is that which is "infected" with human limitations. Thus to reason is to dodge rather than meet the argument that contingency is tantamount to ignorance. But there is a positive basis in good evidence for believing in the reality of objective indeterminism. It can be stated in trenchant terms. Contingency derives from what we do know rather than from what we do not know. It is not a specter arising from the abyss which yawns between facts but an inseparable companion of the facts themselves.[2] Contingency is best attested where our knowledge is most secure. Three related yet separable considerations point the way to the doctrine of contingency: (1) an analysis of the fact of knowing, (2) the method of knowing, and (3) empirical reality as known.

[2] Cf. Paul Tillich, *The Interpretation of History* (New York: Charles Scribner's Sons, 1936), pp. 270–71.

THE FACT OF KNOWING

At first reading this section may seem to support the notion that contingency is another name for ignorance, but the careful reader will readily detect the fact that a much more comprehensive point is being made, namely, that knowledge is always relative to the observer or the knower. This is simply an application of the principle of relativity to the fact of knowing. It would be accepted as a truism to assert that objects are discovered in relation to other objects and never in isolation. But what will not be accepted as truistic is the inevitable development of this position implied in the assertion that knowledge of objects is as revelatory of the knower as of the known. Yet this is the meaning of both Heisenberg's " principle of indeterminacy " and Mead's notion of " objective perspective."

John Dewey translates Heisenberg's famous principle into this somewhat more readable statement: " Heisenberg's principle compels a recognition of the fact that interaction prevents an accurate measurement of velocity and position for *any* body, the demonstration centering about the roles of the interaction of the observer in determining what actually happens. . . . He [Heisenberg] showed that if we fix, metrically, velocity, then there is a range of indeterminateness in the assignment of position, and vice versa. When one is fixed, the other is defined only within a specified limit of probability. The element of indeterminateness is not connected with defect in the method of observation but is intrinsic. The particle observed does not *have* fixed position or velocity, for it is changing all the time because of interaction. . . ." [3]

[3] *The Quest for Certainty*, p. 202. Cf. Spaulding, *op. cit.*, pp. 204 ff., for another exposition of this principle.

Dewey feels that there are three important philosophic implications in this principle: (1) "What is known is seen to be a product in which the act of observation plays a necessary role. Knowing is seen to be a participant in what is finally known." [4] (2) "The metaphysics of existence as something fixed and therefore capable of literally exact mathematical description and prediction is undermined." [5] (3) Scientific laws become "formulae for the prediction of the probability of an observable occurrence." [6]

Mead's notion of "objective perspective" [7] makes a similar assertion about the fact of knowing, though based upon the facts of social rather than physical science. He begins by describing knowledge as a product of a consentient set, which simply means an object or event viewed from a certain perspective. One of the attributes of consciousness and mind is the ability both to attempt to view the world from someone else's consentient set (which can only be by means of an imaginative leap) and to invite others to attempt to see the world as we see it. This endeavor aims to build up an objective perspective, i.e., system of consentient sets. The ancient poem about the six blind men of Hindustani and the elephant is a rough illustration of the point. Each had his own experience, hence his own view, of what the elephant was like: leaf, snake, rope, wall, pillar, spear. Each was wise in believing that his was *a* correct impression. Each was wrong in insisting that his was *the* correct impression. What was needed, instead of loud dispute, was the effort to experience the elephant from the other five "consentient sets."

[4] Op. cit., p. 204.
[5] Ibid., p. 204.
[6] Ibid., p. 206.
[7] G. H. Mead, The Philosophy of the Present (Chicago: Open Court Publishing Co., 1932), pp. 161 ff.

This would have resulted in the construction of an objective perspective of the elephant which would have included the truth in the assertion of each blind man.

Professor C. I. Lewis reinforces this interpretation of the knowing situation in a chapter entitled "The Relativity of Knowledge."[8]   He reaches three important conclusions: (1) Knowledge is relative to an actual or possible mind. (2) Knowledge of reality can be stated only in relative terms, i.e., in terms of the variables involved in the knowing act. (3) If propositions incorporating the relative terms (each blind man's perspective, for example) are validly drawn, they are absolutely rather than relatively true of reality.   But this is not tantamount to saying that any array of such propositions is exhaustive of reality.   Hence what we call knowledge is and must remain partial, though it may be true to the nature of reality in so far as reality has swung into the ken of human experience.

I have given this much space to a summary of the technical appraisals of the fact of knowing because of its profound implications for the doctrine of contingency.   The element of contingency suggested throughout derives not so much from the limitations of human knowing as from the relativistic character of reality as a whole.   Hence it is as inept to decry the partial character of knowledge as it is to lament the relativistic nature of reality.   The former is an instance of the latter.

THE METHOD OF KNOWING

Few persons are prepared to deny the assertion that the most reliable method we have for dealing with empirical reality is that of science.   Critics may disagree as to some

[8] *Mind and the World Order*, chap. 6.

details of it; it may be defined so narrowly as to describe only the physical sciences and rule out as nonscientific social studies however carefully performed. But all are agreed on its basic characteristic, observation and reason — observation of facts in order to discover their "nature," i.e., characteristics which they always exhibit; reason or a determined effort to locate this nature in a system of laws or interrelationships with other and known phenomena. As Cohen points out, the method thrives by cultivating doubts as to the accuracy of its conclusions.[9] It exploits exceptions to the rule in order to discover a stronger rule. It aims to reduce chance to the minimum; its archenemy in the realm of theory is the conception of caprice in nature. Therefore it is usually regarded as the implacable foe of the notion of contingency.

This method is the nerve of scientific procedure. Yet, upon analysis, even it testifies to the reality of contingency or chance in empirical reality. This it does in several ways.[10] In the first place, the method of science does not create the facts with which it works. It discovers them and prides itself upon the fact. But the facts are there prior to the application of the method and they are in an ordered arrangement rather than a hodgepodge. Why should they be there? Whence did they come? Why that order rather than another or none at all? These questions point to an aspect of empirical reality which is as real as discovered data, and the method of science accepts it for what it is. Simply to say that science cannot account for the existence of data does not demonstrate the positive point that contingency is an operative factor in their reality. But it does point out all that is intended, namely, that the most exact method we have for discovering the reason (order) in things must ac-

[9] *Reason and Nature*, p. 85.   [10] *Ibid.*, pp. 151 ff.

cept them for what they are. We shall presently see how Emile Boutroux uses this fact to pave the way to a sweeping assertion about the ultimately contingent character of natural laws.

The second aspect of scientific method which smacks of contingency is the run of interest or attention in the observer which defines the general area of fact or delimits the field within which the solution of the problem lies. In an earlier chapter I have tried to describe the problem solving situation and to point out that the problem up for solution determines what facts are to be accepted or rejected at any given time. That one problem rather than another is controlling observation and reason must be accepted as a contingent fact. True enough, problems grow, as a rule, but even so that they should come to a head in our consciousness under certain specific circumstances is as contingent a fact as is that of the assassination of Ferdinand precipitating the war.

A third type of contingency is found in the general notion of irrelevance. Facts which apparently have no relation to the problem are dismissed as irrelevant. Just what does this mean? And what is their status in the investigation from which they have been ruled out? It is common knowledge that not only great detectives but also great scientists have paid strict attention to some of the admittedly irrelevant facts. Pasteur is an excellent example of this. His researches on the possibility that air might be the carrier of bacteria is only one of many such instances of his scrupulous regard for neglected areas of fact. The real significance of irrelevance for our present purpose is that it is essential to scientific method, which is an exact pursuit along carefully mapped-out lines. Scientific method is an abstracting procedure in that it admits some and rejects most facts on the criterion of relevance. Uneliminable contingency or chance dogs this procedure. True, scientific method will remedy it if it is remedied; witness the case of Pasteur. None the less in terms of any given problem chance is an ineradicable factor.

Another place in the method of science where contingency plays a part is in the moment of discovery. Nor am I, in saying this, forgetting that any significant discovery is based upon profound, comprehensive and rationally rigorous preparation. But I am indicating something well grounded in fact when I say that the occurrence of many discoveries when and where they did occur transcends the rational processes. Take, as example, Lord Hamilton's discovery of a complex mathematical law when he was on a leisurely walk. Or Newton's discovery of the law of gravitation. Both men immediately *verified* their hunches or intuitions by relating them to accepted bodies of theory and fact, but this in no way militates against the reality of chance in the moment of discovery.[11] This will be discussed further in the ensuing section under the broader notion of emergence, in which contingency plays a vital role.

Thus we see that contingency characterizes our most certain knowledge and our most reliable method for securing it. This being true it would seem to be the part of philosophic wisdom to desist from forcing the notion of contingency to bootleg its meanings under the spurious label of ignorance and to give it a license to operate in a respectable manner. This is precisely what a strong movement in contemporary philosophy is doing when it emphasizes the contingent character of empirical reality.

[11] A. D. Ritchie, *Scientific Method* (New York: Harcourt, Brace & Co., 1923), pp. 53 f.: "Induction is an art."

EMPIRICAL REALITY AS KNOWN

The past three centuries have seen a wealth of information about our universe poured out before us by the sciences. Philosophers have been alternately bewildered by the complexity of the offering and busily engaged in piecing together some sort of picture of the whole. It is therefore highly pertinent to our discussion to note that almost every great philosophical system since the beginning of the nineteenth century has allowed ample room for the notion of contingency in its formulation of the nature of existence. It may prove helpful briefly to sketch several such, emphasizing only those aspects which argue for the reality of contingency or objective indeterminism.

One such is the *voluntarism* of Schopenhauer in whose thought reality is a blind surging will to create — something like a blind painter who daubs at a canvas which he cannot see with paints that he himself has mixed. Historically, this view represents a reaction from the lopsided rationalistic determinism of Spinoza and Hegel in whose thought there is always prevision of ends, if not with man, then with God. Schopenhauer's universe is one in which contingency runs amuck.

The *pluralism* of William James is an open and stubborn avowal that reality is not one but many; not unified but diversified; not controlled by an all-inclusive purpose, but the battleground for varieties of purposes. James's thought reflects all too clearly the close of the day of romanticizing the enormous loss and wastage of evolution, the bitter reality of class struggle, and the anguish of personal conflict. For him, the significance of moral choices depended upon the fact of contingency in the universe because of which loss and gain were real and gain was not always vouchsafed him who did his best to choose wisely. This train of reflections is a direct reaction to and repudiation of European and American idealism, which always managed somehow or other to rule chance out of their universes.

The *vitalism* of Henri Bergson contains one of the most trenchant statements of contingency. In fact, taken as a whole, the notion of objective indeterminism plays a larger role in it than in any other contemporary system of thought. For Bergson, scientific, rational knowledge is an abstraction from the full flow of reality. The total thrust of rational knowledge is to create a schematization of empirical phenomena sufficiently deterministic to make those reliable predictions that are essential to practical actions. Within this construct there is no room for contingency, and no wonder, since it is set up with chance as its main antagonist. But such knowledge cannot pretend to describe reality as a whole, which is essentially indeterministic. Bergson's famous phrase *élan vital* is the key to its character. It resembles Schopenhauer's creative activity though it is much more friendly to the notion of universal design. It is important to remember that, for Bergson, the universal flow is genuine creativity, rather than an unfolding of a predetermined purpose.

One of Bergson's older contemporaries was Emile Boutroux. To him we are indebted for one of the earliest attacks on the notion of natural law. His famous doctoral dissertation dealt with the contingency of natural laws.[12] He did not deny the existence of such laws but he did point out that no sound reason can be given for their nature. They might just as well have been of quite a different character. For

[12] *The Contingency of Natural Laws* (Chicago: Open Court Publishing Co., 1920).

example, can anyone give a logically valid reason why the natural laws found by Alice in Wonderland should not obtain in our universe? That they do not is obvious, but is it as obvious that they could not? To reason from the existence of our set of natural laws to the position that they alone are possible is obviously fallacious. The most that can be said in this direction is to point out that the present system of causal relationships was one of perhaps several possible sets and is the one that came to be characteristic of empirical reality. What Boutroux was saying may be illustrated by some such example as this: We have a fertile plot of ground, favorably located climatically. We have in our hands two seeds, an acorn and a squash. If we plant the acorn, the potentialities of the soil and climate express themselves through the deterministic mechanism of the oak. If we had dropped the squash seed, the results would have been quite different. While we would have reasons for dropping one rather than the other, the potentialities of the environment were ready to respond to either. Just so, existence, the world of empirical phenomena, might have been dominated by an entirely different set of natural laws.

Nor has this point of Boutroux's languished unnoticed. Challenging as it did both materialistic and spiritualistic determinism, it came as a shock to science and religion alike. It was a frank denial of their endeavors, not alone to describe phenomena, but also to show why it is inevitable that they should be that way. The classical notion of God as Uncaused Cause, First Cause, was no more and certainly no less severely shaken than Spinoza's substance and the French materialists' notion of universal law. No one has yet met Boutroux's main thesis, which is an out-and-out affirmation of the reality of contingency precisely in that area of empirical phenomena where one would be least likely to look for it — its laws.

E. G. Spaulding is in complete agreement with Boutroux's fundamental contention. "Instances of necessity, i.e., limited 'fields' or realms with which there are 'connections' that are characterized by necessity, I do find, but that the 'occurrence' itself of such fields is necessitated, or that there are necessary connections between these 'fields,' I do not find." [13] While Morris Cohen is of the same opinion,[14] he proceeds to apply the principle of polarity and thereby balances the irrational or contingent aspect of the universe with the rational and determinate characteristics. This gives him a much firmer grasp on the possibility of solution. In summarizing this chapter we shall make more of this observation. Just now we must get a glimpse of the meaning of contingency in connection with the widespread notion of emergence and novelty.

Professor A. N. Whitehead's comprehensive philosophy makes much of the indeterminateness of the future: that is, what is future is really future, hence unactualized. Any given event is a cluster of potentialities, some of which will be actualized in the form of some succeeding present. Movement from the past through the present into the future is real, but the precise nature of that future is strictly indeterminate prior to its crystallization in a concrete present. Obviously the doctrine of contingency can and does loom large at this juncture in Professor Whitehead's thought. Just why and the extent to which some possibilities are realized is not determinable either ahead of time or with completeness

[13] Spaulding, *op. cit.*, pp. v, 104 ff. Cf. also Stebbings, *Introduction to Logic*, p. 201: "The system of the actual world *cannot* be logically necessary, and anything that is the case might have been other than it is." (Quoted by Spaulding, p. 86.)

[14] *Op. cit.*, pp. 151–52.

afterward. That some possibilities rather than others have become concrete presents is a fact, but *why* some rather than others cannot be determined in advance of the fact because the very nature of the fact is as yet indeterminate.

George Herbert Mead's provocative discussion of "an emergent" and "the present" deserves careful consideration at this point in our discussion. For him not only the future but also the *past* is contingent.

By an emergent or a present Mead means a novel event, one that is recognizably different from something else. Change is incontestably operative in the emergence of a present. New factors are there too or it would be indistinguishable from the preceding present. An example might be selected from any field, since for Mead any object, fact or sensation constitutes a present. The emergence of a new structure in biology as mutation, or in the mind as a gripping idea, or in religion as conversion, one and all illustrate what is meant by a present. Although difficulties in exposition are greater when one attempts a complicated illustration, the victory, if won, is of greater value to the understanding both of the immediate and of the broader problem. Before invoking an incident from the life of Paul to clarify the meaning of an emergent, it will be well for us to set up a general logical device or diagram by which the explanation will proceed (which diagram can be used to fit any other present).

The diagram: Suppose we wish to understand present X. Upon analysis of it (X), we discover that processes A, B, and C were responsible for its creation as emergent. Hence the past of X is A, B, and C. Let us now suppose that an emergence occurs by virtue of which X is transformed into Y. Now we have an emergent, a new present, a novelty, which must be explained. It is obviously in error to reason that

A, B, and C condition Y in the same way that they conditioned X. If this were true, there would be no difference between X and Y. But there is a novel element in Y that must be explained. Analysis of Y reveals that in addition to X (as emergent of A, B, and C) other factors, D, E, and F, are operative units in its past. Hence the past of Y is X, D, E, and F. But this past did not exist *as past* prior to the emergence of Y. Mead is clear on this point: " The past of an event is not just an antecedent present." [15]

The concrete example: One of the emergents or presents in Paul's life was his consuming hatred for the Christians which expressed itself in the zeal with which he persecuted them. Let this stand for the X in the preceding paragraph. Upon analysis of it we find certain definite factors which largely produced it: A — his Pharisaical training, stressing obedience to the Law as the way to righteousness; B — the social, political and religious situation at Jerusalem; and C — his own violent personal reaction to all who disagreed with him. Shortly after X became a fact it gave way to a second emergent, Y — Paul's conversion to the Christian faith. Obviously this is a novelty, a present, which demands another explanation. It is radically different from X, yet obviously related to it. Analysis of Y reveals the fact that in addition to X (Paul's hatred for Christians) certain other factors loom large in the emergent: D — Stephen's martyrdom under the stones cast by the mob led by Paul; E — a brooding over the fact of sin which all his zeal in good works could neither erase nor lessen; and F — the faith of Christians not only that Jesus provides release from sin but also that he fulfills and supplants the Law as the way of righteousness. Hence the past of Y is X, D, E, and F. Relative to this and

[15] *Op. cit.*, pp. xvii, 13.

every other complex present or emergent, conditioning factors may be added or subtracted, with adequate cause, without invalidating the general tenor of the argument or modifying the conclusions.

Both the logical diagram and the concrete example lead, upon reflection, to some significant considerations: (1) Any given present at one and the same time exemplifies scientific determinism, yet is a novelty, an emergent. It is an example of scientific determinism, because, ideally at least, it lends itself to complete explanation in terms of law. But — and this is its novelty — the character of its determinism is its own. That is to say, these factors were not operative in any prior present; there is no place other than *this* emergent where they are found in *this* combination. "The determinism then holds of the past implied in any present, the emergence in the relation of one such present, with its past, to another." [16]

(2) Science is related to an emergent in two ways. First, it cannot predict an emergent prior to its emergence in the form of a present. Second, once an emergent is actualized, science can measure it, analyze it into its component parts, or describe its meanings until we feel familiar with it. The purpose of science's endeavor is to enable it to "previse the future." [17]

Parenthetically, one of Mead's unresolved difficulties enters precisely at this juncture. For how can the future emergent be "prevised" by any knowledge of the past, however complete? No amount of knowledge of X in Paul's case would have enabled one to predict Y, and for exactly the reason assigned by Mead, namely, the insertion of new factors into the situation, which coalesced with X to produce Y.

[16] *Ibid.*, p. xviii.　　　　　[17] *Ibid.*, p. 331.

The solution to this perplexity is, it seems to me, suggested by Morris Cohen's rigorous use of the principle of polarity when dealing with the problem of constancy and change. For him, there is a persistence of invariant relations and rational structure together with profound modifications in the character of details throughout the chain of emergents. Cohen likewise insists that scientific method is successful precisely because it both assumes this and is a self-correcting system of revealing with increasing accuracy the nature of this underlying structure. Although Mead would be prompt to dismiss the suggestion as "rationalistic metaphysics" I am of the opinion that it has definite bearing on his thought. The matter might be summarized this way: There are necessary relations which run through past, present and future; such relations rise to the surface or become concreted in presents; it is the task of science to discover these relations and to trace them *backward* in the conviction that a better understanding of their nature yields a more valid prediction of the future. Only upon some such basis can science be at all relevant to the future.

Even with this modification Mead continues to be the most careful analyst of the meaning of "emergent." It is, therefore, in order to summarize his conclusions and relate them to the notion of contingency.

(1) Two strains of influence enter into the structure of any emergent. One is the preceding present with a fixed character by virtue of which it was itself known as an emergent. Hence this deterministic system of factors enters as a certain, predictable, known factor into the construction of its successor. Naturally all thought of time and space would vanish and the Parmenidean One would be accepted as descriptive of reality if the preceding present were the only

source of conditioning, since all emergents would be alike, hence indistinguishable.

But another set of factors streams in from an utterly unpredictable angle and exerts an unpredictable influence on the emerging present. Why they should come, we have no way of knowing. Nor do we know that they have come, much less what they are, until the present which they condition becomes a full-blown emergent. Then we can ferret out its component parts and separate the two strains of conditioning which comprise it.

Two corollaries ensue. One is that the past is contingent. What the past of a given present is, science can determine to some degree — ideally, of course, completely. But what the nature of *this* past (that of Y, for example) was while the preceding present (X) with its past held sway, not even omniscience could determine. And that because of the plain fact that the component parts of any past are indecipherable until the present they condition has emerged and has thereby incorporated them into a substance or event with definite structure.

The second corollary is that the future is contingent. Just what factors will impinge upon the structure of the present to produce an emergent is indeterminate. Certain is it that each emergent derives its uniqueness from contingent factors. Science may know with meticulous accuracy the laws and relations which dominate each present and which enter into the conditioning of the future, yet not be able to predict with more than statistical accuracy the character and direction of the future, because the unique, hence deterministic, features in the new structure derive from unpredictable sources.[18]

[18] Cf. Cohen, *op. cit.*, p. 137.

(2) The emergent quality of the universe confronts science with uneliminable contingency because the laws which characterize any present emergent will be revised in unknown and unknowable ways when the future emergent arrives. Let us be clear about this point: The laws of the past present are not scrapped with the passing of their present. Rather they are modified by and adjusted to the new factors. But science must build upon the assumption of change as well as of uniformity. There is no way to insure the permanency of the structure of any present. If what is recorded in the history of science is a reliable index as to the nature of scientific laws, they are in process of continual restatement due to the contingent character of past and future alike. To reason thus is not to impugn the validity of science as the most accurate way to know the present and to construct its past. Nor is it to argue that there is any other and more reliable way to previse the future. If this could be done, scientific method would do it because such prevision rests on knowledge of continuing laws and relations, and science is our most trustworthy way of knowing and applying these. But neither science nor any other enterprise can control either the nature or the results of the contingent factors which are as characteristic of empirical reality as are structured relations. William James's dream of a wide-open world has come true in Mead's philosophy of the present.

SUMMARY

Contingency is a real factor in empirical reality. But contingency alone is meaningless. Pure chaos would not call attention to itself. Contingency has significance only when viewed as the polar opposite of determinism. Both are equally true aspects of empirical reality. Determinism, alone, is as useless a concept as contingency taken by itself. One cannot be explained or understood without the other, yet they sustain a contradictory, at least a paradoxical relationship to each other.

When Bergson and Spaulding would make contingency more fundamental than determinate order it seems to me they are in error. Each admits that both concepts are descriptive of portions of reality, yet for specific reasons argues for the ultimacy of contingency. Whereas their arguments for the reality of contingency derive from empirical reality, their reasons for the ultimacy of contingency are drawn from some area, either intuitional or logical, outside of empirical fact.

Cohen balances the irrational or contingent aspects of existence with the rational. Both are valid as description and, so far as we know, are ultimate categories. Mead balances contingency or unpredictability with determinism or rational order, regarding them as of equal value and validity.

Therefore, I am of the opinion that any discipline, whether art, science or religion, purporting to appreciate, discover or describe certain aspects of the world of facts, must keep a careful eye on the fact of contingency. To be obsessed by it is to lose all notion of purpose and to cling to the specious moment which willy-nilly fades away; to ignore it is to hypostatize purposes into an all-inclusive Purpose and eventually to crystallize it into a comforting dogmatism.

Tentativeness, as I have indicated, is enforced open-mindedness. Whether we like it or not we are part and parcel of a universe which is not of a single piece. Echoes of cosmic strife are continually borne to listening ears. We frequently feel the struggle within ourselves, agreeing with Paul that ours is a " living death." What the larger implications for religion are remains to be considered. Just now it is sufficient to say that our universe has at work in it an element of real chance which is attested by what we know rather than by what we do not know.

VII

SCIENTIFIC HYPOTHESIS AND RELIGIOUS BELIEF

THERE ARE not wanting those that might agree that tentativeness is indispensable to scientific method, yet categorically deny that it has any place in religious belief. And the precise reason for this discrimination is not hard to find: an unbridgeable chasm yawns between a scientific hypothesis and a religious belief. They are different not merely in degree, as I have implied, but actually in kind. Upholders of this point of view have advanced several types of distinctions which are important because they are instructive of the nature of the most widely used solution of the conflict between science and religion. I propose to state and enlarge upon two such attempts at division of labor between these two great disciplines.

It is argued that science and religion deal with different though related problems. Scientific hypothesis deals with the detailed circumference problems of life; religious belief dwells in the center of the life enterprise. Religion is the custodian of purpose, immediate and pluralized as well as ultimate and unified. It aims to provide a perspective on life *in toto* and cannot fairly be broken up into segments. The reverse is true of science; it proceeds by division and subdivision of problems which, though broad in scope at the outset, are solved, if solved, by a multitude of investigations of isolated problems. Cancer is a tragic human problem and is all too broad in scope. Scientists the world over are attacking it by means of every conceivable approach — some via heredity, others through food, still others through infection and injury. Few scenes fill one with greater respect for the potentialities of the human race than these tens of thousands of persons in laboratories throughout the world studying the cells and tissues of rats, rabbits and men. If the problem of cancer is ever solved it will be through such patient detailed investigations to which tentativeness is life itself because their scientific hypotheses must be mobile.

But cancer does not affect human life simply as a physiological phenomenon which can be analyzed and attacked piecemeal. It likewise strikes life as a whole, necessitates a rearrangement of the total enterprise — in short, induces suffering. The problem of suffering is distinctly a religious one. True, the causes of suffering, if organic, may be understood by scientific procedure; but the agony of life as a whole is an inevitable result, and in our present world there is an abundance of it owing to social as well as organic causes, and religion alone attempts to minister to those who bear it. Some religions counsel escape from it, either by denying its reality as Christian Science does or by advising the transferring of all one's affections to life after death where peace alone will reign. Others urge men to bear up courageously, either in the name of posterity or because of a God who will not suffer men to be tempted beyond that which they can endure. Yet the central fact of suffering is this: it colors the whole of life whenever it is characteristic of life. It cannot be segregated. It infects purposes, desires and loyalties. Any attempt to deal with it in detail must recognize this inclusive nature. In other words, the problem of suffering is different in kind from the problem of cancer. Therefore any method of dealing with it must minister to the whole of it.

John Oman asserts that the nature of the reality to be investigated determines the character of the method to be employed.[1] If you are dealing with an aspect of reality, use science, but if you would learn of the whole, religion alone can aid you. Only the prevalence of some such attitude can account for the fact which Whitehead calls to our attention, namely, that modification of a scientific theory is hailed as an advance in science, but a change in religious belief betokens a reverse for religion.[2]

Professor W. H. Bernhardt has recently given this general outlook a new and significant phrasing. Scientific hypothesis, he urges, deals with manipulable materials; religious belief is concerned with nonmanipulable problems. Religion deals with the crises of life which come whether or no. Scientific method is useless when confronted by the problem of death. Yet religion must have a message for this and other extremities of the human spirit. Therefore, science can proceed by rational hypothecation and verification, whereas religion is animated by intuitions born of faith, which, for all its definite historical background, never loses its genius as essentially faith, that is, confidence in conclusions derived from intuition rather than from scientific method.[3]

Another attempt to reconcile science and religion by separating responsibility holds that scientific hypothesis and religious belief are different in that they travel different roads to truth. Whereas the former uses cultivation of doubt to secure greater truth, the latter uses an act of faith. Scientific hypothesis utilizes the logical structure of doubt, the " if-

[1] *Natural and Supernatural*, pp. 108 ff.
[2] *Science and the Modern World* (New York: The Macmillan Co., 1923), pp. 270 f.
[3] W. H. Bernhardt, " The Significance of the Changing Function of Religion," *Journal of Religion*, Oct., 1932, pp. 556 ff.

then" framework. The most it can ever affirm is that *if* this is so, *then* something else follows. Religious belief, on the other hand, proceeds by the attitude of acceptance through faith alone, epitomized by the famous passage, " Though He slay me, yet will I trust Him." In these days we are prone to laugh at the *credo quia absurdum* of the Schoolmen; yet they were only recognizing the logical extremity to which reliance upon faith is inevitably driven. While we no longer *say,* " I believe that which is absurd," many widely held religious beliefs prove that we actually do believe something very like it.

Another way to put the dilemma is this: Science stakes its existence upon the ability and validity of observation and reason to reach truth or to come as near reaching it as is humanly possible in this world of change. Religion need not oppose reason, may even embrace it, but never wholly places its fundamental beliefs under reason's care, for their trusted guardian is faith born of authority of some kind or other. There are some things we simply cannot reason about with profit because the facts which reason demands are lacking, yet these matters are too important to pass by without an affirmation. Therefore, say many, religious belief born of faith not only is necessary but is likewise competent to supply the desired affirmations. Professor D. C. Macintosh argues with clarity and cogency that we are entitled to believe as true all that is essential to moral action.[4]

It is patent that we must determine, if possible, the nature of religious belief before we can fairly and with profit insist that tentativeness is as germane to it as to scientific hypothesis. John Dewey sounds the keynote of our venture

[4] *The Reasonableness of Christianity* (New York: Charles Scribner's Sons, 1925).

when he asserts that one of the two burning questions which
modern liberalism in religion has not yet faced but must
eventually face if it would clarify its position is: " What is
the place of belief in religion and by what methods is true
belief achieved and tested? " [5]   It is significant that all contemporary attempts to answer this question proceed by
way of contrasting religious belief with or relating it to scientific hypothesis. The four attempts which I am going to
present have been selected because they are in some measure
representative of contemporary movements of thought about
and in religion.

BELIEF AS REVELATION OF REALITY

The precise status of belief in the family of possible relations to an idea has always been elusive. The Council of
Trent endeavored to fasten it down, and the dubious result
appears in the definition: " The word ' believe ' . . . does
not here [Apostles' Creed] mean ' to think,' ' to imagine,'
' to be of opinion,' but, as the Sacred Scriptures teach, it expresses the deepest conviction of the mind, by which we
give a firm and unhesitating assent to God revealing his
mysterious truths." [6]
The great traditions in Protestantism and Catholicism
agree that religious belief must be accepted as revelation of
reality.[7] Revelation covers both the content and the method
by which it is ascertained. Although there is wide disagreement as to the validity of different methods (church, Bible,
mystical experience), all agree that the content of their particular revelations is an accurate portrayal or description of

---

[5] *Characters and Events,* II, 458.
[6] *Catechism of the Council of Trent* (London: Keatings and Browne, 1829),
p. 12.
[7] Cf. Chap. II.

reality — accurate in the sense that it cannot be improved upon; it is final truth.

Sigmund Freud not only accepts this as the correct conception of religious belief but, with it as basis, proceeds to demonstrate that religion is an illusion.[8] We shall see that when one questions the validity of this conception of the nature of belief he has laid the ax at the roots of Freud's polemic against religion. Consider his central thesis that religious doctrines (that which is *believed*) " are all illusions, they do not admit of proof and no one can be compelled to consider them as true or to believe in them. Some of them are so improbable, so very incompatible with everything we have laboriously discovered about the reality of the world, that we may compare them — taking adequately into account the psychological differences — to delusions. Of the reality value of most of them we cannot judge; just as they cannot be proved, neither can they be refuted." [9] Religious beliefs originate in wishful thinking, in wanting something so badly that the very intensity of desire is construed to guarantee its reality. They deal with the most profound puzzles which confront us, yet they claim to possess the solution. But beliefs do not remain in the thin air of speculation; they insert themselves in human lives not as hypotheses but as reliable predications of reality. They become part of a social milieu and a historical tradition. They suffuse the culture of whole civilizations with their ideology. They raise up a compact inner circle (church) which guards them from impious hands and calls all men to accept their light and leading.

But — and this is the cutting edge of Freud's case — re-

---

[8] *The Future of an Illusion* (London: Horace Liveright, 1928).

[9] *Ibid.*, p. 55.

ligious beliefs are incapable of rational, experimental testing. If you cannot accept them as true, bolstered as they are only by tradition and authority, then you will reject them as illusions. Now an "illusion need not be necessarily false, that is to say, unrealizable or incompatible with reality." [10] But it is incapable of exact proof and for the most part is not approachable by scientific procedure. [11] It is patent that, in Freud's thought, religious belief and any kind of *investigation* of reality are sworn enemies. Scientific belief has the whole truth or at least as much of it as is open to humanity. Religious belief is the creation of psychological compensation and tradition and is the ward of authority. Its value and potency are directly proportionate to the blindness with which people accept its claim to revealed knowledge of reality. It can be neither proved nor disproved. It is above the canons by which proof and disproof operate. It is and must remain uncompromisingly opposed to any other effort to approach reality. Hence there is a conflict in which no quarter is desired between religious belief and the scientific attitude of investigation by experimentation.

That this conception of belief is commonly held is attested by the widespread efforts to show by fair arguments or foul that there is no *real* conflict between what science finds and what religion teaches. It fits in with Whitehead's observation, previously mentioned, that modification of theories is a recognized essential to the growth of science while change in religious belief betokens another defeat for religion. This must remain true so long as the vitality of religious belief is dependent upon the inerrancy of its knowledge of reality. If religious belief is regarded as revelation of reality, there

[10] *Ibid.*, p. 54.   [11] *Ibid.*, p. 94.

is no place in it for tentativeness, which religion is obliged to regard as an implacable enemy.[12]

Whereas Freud openly accepts the position that religious belief is antithetical to scientific procedure and decides against it on that basis, William Adams Brown endeavors to restore the prestige of religious belief by showing wherein it is similar to scientific procedure. He recognizes the fact, which seems not to have caught Freud's attention, that religious beliefs wax and wane, grow and decay, live and die, much like scientific hypotheses. But through all these fluctuations of belief we clearly see certain fundamental postulates which do not change for either. The postulates of science, according to Dr. Brown, are " that there is an order in nature which expresses the way in which things may be counted upon to happen; that man has capacity within limits to understand what that order is; and that scientific method is the way in which trustworthy knowledge of that order is to be gained." [13] The postulates or assumptions of religion are: " First . . . there is a moral and spiritual order which is no less real than the aspect of reality made known to us through the senses. . . . A second assumption is that the divine, which is also the excellent, has been made known to men in definite and recognizable ways so that we may be sure not only that deity exists but also within limits what it is like. . . . A third assumption . . . is that *a trustworthy knowledge of God is made possible to man by his capacity to act upon his ideals,*

---

[12] D. E. Trueblood, *The Spiritual Essence of Religion* (New York: Harper & Bros., 1936), does not escape this fixity of belief by his notion of " continuous revelation." Religious belief continues to have a superior ingress into the profundities of reality and yields truths beyond testing.

[13] William Adams Brown, *Pathways to Certainty,* p. 206.

so that when he trusts and follows that which is most excellent, he enters into communion with deity." [14]

But these postulates alone do not satisfy religious cravings for specificity any more than those of science satisfy a multitude of concrete needs, i.e., need to know cause of diseases, depressions, etc. The thrust for a more exact and fuller knowledge takes the form of hypotheses for religion and science alike. Take, for example, the first postulate of religion (which Dr. Brown equates with God) that there is a moral and spiritual order which is no less real than the aspect of reality made known to us through the senses. Hypotheses as to the fuller nature of this order are necessary. Hence we have the several which underlie various religions such as Christianity, Buddhism and Mohammedanism. "Our hypothesis concerning God defines that part of our thought about God which has not yet been completely verified by experiment and which is therefore capable of progressive redefinition." [15] But you do not change or alter the postulate. That is fixed and certain. Whether or not a hypothesis is a reliable amplification is open to question; it must be held tentatively. The procedure by which verification takes place is that of experiment in daily living.

Dr. Brown is frankly empirical in his statement that " God is the subject of experiment in religion in the same sense in which nature is the subject of experiment in science. And as the hypotheses of the different sciences sum up our knowledge of nature to date and define the issues on which further inquiry is necessary, so the doctrines of religion sum up men's experience of God up to date and define the issues on which further experiment is necessary." [16]

Hence we see that the doctrines of religion, that beliefs

[14] *Ibid.*, p. 209 (Brown's italics).   [15] *Ibid.*   [16] *Ibid.*, p. 210.

about the postulate of God are as provisional as they are in-dispensable. This conception of religious belief might be accepted as openly friendly to the notion of tentativeness were it not for the steady tendency on Dr. Brown's part to attribute the certainty due postulates to notions which defi-nitely are hypotheses and should be held tentatively.[17] For example, he urges that the faith of theistic religion is that there is a wiser mind and stronger will for good than ours at work in the universe.[18] In another connection he insists that this core of reality is " akin to man though infinitely wiser and better." [19] Now, by definition, these ought to be religious beliefs rather than postulates, held tentatively rather than certainly; they ought to be regarded as hypotheses which define the course of future experimentation and there-fore held tentatively until validated. But Dr. Brown regards them as certain truths. This continual and covert crowding of hypotheses or beliefs into postulates gives birth to the sus-picion that the line between them is not always evident. This is obviously the case in Dr. Brown's summary rejection of the notion that the idea of tentativeness enters in any way into the relationship between the worshiper and his God. He quotes with disapproval E. A. Burtt's notion that one ought to be tentative about " even the noblest ideas and the most appealing emotions that come to [him] from [his] own particular heritage," and H. N. Wieman when he writes that " the apologist for religion should present all our most sacred beliefs and programs of actions as tentative and exper-imental." [20] Just why Dr. Brown should disagree with these

[17] I think the fatal weakness in Dr. Brown's quest for certainty is the analogy between the postulates of science and religion and his attribution of certainty to them precisely because they are incapable of proof (*ibid.*, p. 206).

[18] *Ibid.*, p. 193.

[19] *Ibid.*, p. 41.   [20] *Ibid.*, pp. 210–11 (footnote).

sentiments is not easy to see unless he is not clear in his own thought on what is postulate and what hypothesis. Certainty can come to the hypothesis only through verification, which in the case of religious beliefs is always very uncertain. A belief is not certain simply because it purports to amplify a postulate. All beyond postulate is hypothetical and tentative. If Dr. Brown had consistently adhered to this notion of religious belief it would be easier to estimate his contribution to the solution of the problematical relations between science and religion.

BELIEF AS APPROXIMATION TO REALITY

History and sociology loom large in Dean Shailer Mathews' analysis of religious belief. His thought on this subject differs from Dr. Brown's in two important respects: (1) he does not proceed by analogy with science, and (2) he keeps beliefs in a consistently mobile or plastic state, in which growth is not only possible but inevitable. There is no vacillation in his position. He is in avowed opposition to the notion that religious beliefs are revelations of reality. Beliefs do represent the most reliable approximations which a given age could make to reality. The very nature of religion requires this. For him, " in its ultimate nature the behavior represented by the word religion can be described as a phase of the life process which seeks by control or cooperation to get help from those elements of its cosmic environment upon which men feel themselves dependent by setting up social, that is, personal relations with them." [21]

Theology as the rational expression and coherent systematization of religious beliefs is functional rather than the

[21] Mathews, *The Growth of the Idea of God* (New York: The Macmillan Co., 1931), p. 6.

custodian of perfect and finished truths. Its purpose is to place traditional values at the disposal of contemporary life. It is not solely conservator of inherited experiences of value; it is also interpreter of them. Therefore it borrows from any given age patterns capable of transmitting its felt values. Now a " pattern is a social institution or practice used to give content and intelligibility to otherwise unrationalized beliefs." [22] Different ages will have different dominant institutions and will provide different patterns for religious beliefs. Dean Mathews points out how the doctrine of the atonement has been transmitted by means of eight different patterns. In other words, the doctrines of religions are functional and upon analysis fall into two distinct parts which are never separated in actual living. First, the doctrine has a traditional value, a basic message which is its *raison d'être,* apart from which it simply would not have existed. This value is never found in its naked reality. It is found in part in certain types of experience and is expressed by means of them. Second, the contemporary expression of it, which is relative to the social situation of a given age. The process by which a new pattern displaces an older form is never a conscious one but is an inevitable development of changed social conditions. Doctrines are not the creation of idle moments of whimsical fancy. Each one is an endeavor to answer a specific problem, to release a certain tension by indicating a value the discovery and appropriation of which would solve the problem or release the tension.

Doctrines so conceived cease to be subjective playthings and become as objective an aspect of a social situation as its form of government. They must meet a rigid test which is an inexorable requirement. Dean Mathews says that the test by

[22] Mathews, *The Atonement and the Social Process,* p. 25.

which the truth of any doctrine is determined is " its capacity to vindicate the deepest faith and the moral conduct of that group of Christians by which it was drawn up." [23]   Which, as I understand it, is saying that inherited conceptions of value must be related to problematic situations in such a way that order and purpose replace disorder and hesitation. The test of a religious belief, then, is its ability to provide direction for living. Granting the obvious point that " deepest faith " and " moral conduct " elude precise definition, the fact can hardly be disputed that each one *indicates* certain distinct areas of fact which are susceptible of a more accurate, at least fuller, description. Doctrines are vital only so long as they give expression to the values which undergird faith and action. Certainly the value of doctrines begins and ends with their vitality. The most important thing about them is what they are trying to say, the enduring reality which gives relevance and compulsion to all expressions of it, that fact which is repeatedly, albeit blunderingly, experienced in life and which one endeavors correctly to describe and account for. " Theology will change, but Christian experience and faith embodied in the Christian movement will continue." [24]

Dr. Mathews' thought on religious belief might be summarized this way: (1) Religious beliefs are patterns drawn from the social situations and cannot be understood apart from this background; (2) patterns both *indicate* an experienced value and endeavor to conceptualize it by likening it to other accepted and conceptualized forms of experience; (3) the experienced value is indicated not confined by the conceptualization; (4) new and changing experiences of this value (love, for example) reveal new facts or aspects of it, hence our knowledge of it grows with our experience, social

[23] *Ibid.*, pp. 12–13.   [24] *Ibid.*, pp. 28–29.

as well as personal; and (5) beliefs must be sensitive to cultural shifts and endeavor to keep in an organic relationship a constant experience of value, traditional formulations of it, and that conceptualization of it best calculated to describe and commend it to men.

Tentativeness is essential to the efficacy of belief so conceived. It sets a premium on that attitude toward beliefs which invites change in the interest of a more effective conceptualization of the underlying value. This conception of religious belief utilizes the principle of polarity involved in the terms "certainty" and "tentativeness." Certainty derives from the value experience which is an unmistakably present reality, albeit vaguely cognized by belief. Belief is an attempt to reveal the nature of the underlying value by likening it to known objects. Tentativeness is inevitable because the belief is an approximation of the reality encountered in experience.

Dr. Henry N. Wieman openly espouses the notion that the religious man must regard his beliefs as a scientist regards his hypotheses. "The apologist for religion should present all our most sacred beliefs and programs of action as tentative and experimental." [25] This assertion is such an open invitation to tentativeness that one wonders whether there is any basis for certainty. Dr. Wieman's critics have directed their sharpest attacks at this aspect of his thought. To most of them his attitude, faithfully portrayed in this statement, is throwing out the baby (conviction) with the bath (dogmatism). An examination of certain aspects of his thought will be instructive.

Religion is theocentric. Religious beliefs, all of them, are ultimately statements about "that structure of existence and

[25] Quoted by W. A. Brown, *op. cit.*, pp. 210–11 (footnote).

possibility which sustains and promotes value." Theology, historically speaking, records man's interpretation of what the fuller nature of this structure or God really is. But Dr. Wieman is explicit on the point that religion is not simply a mastery of theology, however sound. Religion is complete devotion to God, and this is something inclusive of but much more comprehensive than an intellectual enterprise. Man first meets God not in theology but in practical action. The " grace of God " comes to the one who strives to live for him rather than to one who strives to master more beliefs about him. Man is not made religious by knowledge about the actuality which sustains, promotes and constitutes greatest value (God), but " what makes a man religious is to make this actuality the supreme concern of his living, no matter how little he may know about it, only knowing that it is." [26]

All of which simply puts in proper perspective the significant place which belief occupies in Dr. Wieman's thought. It has a precise function and nature. To begin with, he dispenses with the notion that it is a fixed and final revelation of reality.[27] He not only reiterates but accepts the challenge thrown out by John Dewey to clarify the nature of belief and its place in religion and to specify the method by which its truth and falsity are achieved. This he does by characterizing it in the following ways.

(1) Belief is the cognitive side of religion. Without it devotion would be an amorphous mass of sentiment. With it loyalties become definite in direction, purposes are possible, and actual discoveries are imminent. Belief, for Wieman as for Mathews, is a synthesis of past experiences of value and suggests the direction of further research in life. As such it

[26] " Theocentric Religion," *Religion in Life,* I, 102.
[27] *Ibid.,* p. 103, and in various other writings.

must keep pace with the experiences of daily living, analyzing, relating and evaluating them.

(2) Belief is tested as is any other cognitive enterprise, i.e., by observation and reason, which means " that method of ruthless criticism and implacable reason which makes every proposition submitted to it progressively self-corrective." [28] Dr. Wieman utterly rejects the right of authorities such as church or Bible to settle a controversial point or to issue fiats relative to inconclusive experiences. Beliefs are to religion what hypotheses are to science and must be tested by precisely the same canons of truth.

(3) Belief is hypothesis. It must include (in the sense of giving some recognition to) the relevant facts. If it does not meet this preliminary requirement it is not a fair hypothesis. But in addition it must point the direction to data as yet unobserved. Innumerable analogies from science present themselves. Perhaps the periodic table of elements is most apt. The known elements are arranged in such a structure that they predict definite characteristics of those elements which have, as yet, eluded observation. A hypothesis without direction and prediction is a contradiction in terms. Just so with religious belief. It not only summarizes known relevant data but must have a definite " lean " toward the future.

Dr. Wieman summarizes his position on belief in this significant statement: " To be sure we must have guiding propositions about it [the object of supreme devotion]. We must have the truest and most adequate propositions we can possibly achieve. We must give our lives and the centuries to the development of such propositions, not for the sake of the propositions in themselves, but because we must have

[28] *Is there a God?* by H. N. Wieman, D. C. Macintosh and M. C. Otto (Chicago: Willett, Clark & Co., 1932), p. 51.

intellectual tools with which to dedicate our lives to God; and we want the best tools that can be had. But always our hearts must be given not to our propositions, but to the reality itself, no matter how different this most worthful object may be from what our propositions assert." [29]

Tentativeness is indispensable if beliefs are to function properly. They are instruments, tools. When they no longer serve either adequately to summarize known relevant data or to direct investigation they are to be discarded carefully though quickly. There is no knowledge of God without beliefs. Hence correct beliefs are one of the crying needs of religion. They alone furnish light and leading for religious living. Yet the driving power in religion is devotion rather than beliefs. Unless religion can elicit deathless devotion it is a doomed and mean affair.[30] "The religion of infallible devotion must take the place of the religion of infallible beliefs." [31] Devotion, then, is the basis of certainty and provides the polar opposite of tentativeness. Tentativeness derives from cognition, certainty from devotion. Religion is the resultant of this tension in the area of values.

We have been surveying two possible positions relative to the nature of religious belief: (1) it is a revelation of reality; (2) it is an approximation of reality. The implications of each for the notion of tentativeness are plain. If religious devotion is dependent upon inerrancy of belief, tentativeness must be rejected root and branch, for it is the death of religion. If religious loyalty is elicited by and trained upon an unknown best found in but not cognized by experience, tentativeness is an invaluable aid in the search for knowledge of

[29] *Ibid.*, p. 85.
[30] Wieman feels that there are definite ways in which such devotion can be elicited. *Is There a God?* p. 128.
[31] *Ibid.*, p. 52.

the object of religious loyalty.   In this case, tentativeness releases religion from the locked hands of dead belief.

TENTATIVENESS AND CERTAINTY IN RELIGIOUS BELIEF

Religion is an empirical enterprise in that the propositions about God, the world and man have at least one empirical fact which makes them relevant to human life.   Its propositions, doctrines or beliefs are assertions as to the ultimate nature or meanings of empirical facts.   The accuracy and value of its theology, then, are in genuine measure dependent upon the realism and insight which it shows within this world of empirical reality.   It must have easily recognizable relevance to life.   When theologians talk about sin they must produce in their audience a sense of pertinence similar in kind to that secured by Jonathan Edwards in his Northampton revival sermons.   When they discourse on love or any other Christian virtue it must be first and foremost of the earth earthy and then of the heaven heavenly.   The subject matter of religious belief is always within the reach of human minds because it is drawn from the context of human life and endeavors to meet specific problems by the advancement of concrete proposals.

If one holds that religious belief is a revelation of reality, he is asserting, indirectly, that we possess certain rather than probable knowledge of empirical reality.   Yet our survey of this problem showed the impossibility of this.   Certain knowledge is prescriptive, whereas empirical knowledge is always descriptive.   Certain knowledge proceeds by means of an invariant relation, whereas empirical knowledge has been, as yet, unable to set up and maintain even the most general type of boundaries between various fields of research.   The only conclusion open to us is that empirical knowledge is probable rather than certain. If religious belief is empirical, or incorporates empirical facts, it cannot lay claim to more than probable knowledge unless the further position is taken that religion possesses a unique way of knowing empirical reality and can therefore claim certain knowledge.[32]

If, on the other hand, one accepts the position I have been outlining, that religious belief is an approximation of reality, he is accepting and abiding by the notion that empirical knowledge is probable rather than certain. Tentativeness is an inevitable concomitant of this conception of religious belief. Religious belief is held tentatively in precisely the same sense as is a scientific hypothesis. The certainties of past experience and experienced reality enter into both types of investigation.

As I shall use the term, "religious attitude" amounts roughly to what Dr. Wieman calls devotion. It is the totality of one's religious response. So conceived it includes both belief and ethical conduct. Religious belief and religious living are integral aspects of the religious attitude. Yet it contains something else which is not adequately expressed by either of these, namely, a loyalty or devotion to an objective reality which is deeper than belief and action though it finds concrete empirical expression in them.

Religion, as Hoffding pointed out, is preeminently concerned with value. It seems to me that this affirmation provides a clue to a significant interpretation of the genius of the religious attitude — that of appreciation of value, or, better still, reverence for value.[33] Were it not for this under-

---

[32] Chap. IV is an endeavor to analyze possible methods by which this is attempted.

[33] Albert Schweitzer's "reverence for life" (*Christendom*, I, No. 1) is in reality a reverence for certain qualities or values found in life.

lying attitude, questions as to specific values would never arise. Stated in its most general terms (so general, in fact, that it is less a belief than an attitude), the religious attitude affirms that relative to life the universe possesses value. It is the basic motivation in the quest for the good, the abundant life. Though specific notions of what constitutes the abundant life may and do change, the notion that there is an abundant life is constant. It always expresses itself in concrete proposals which are up for criticism and experimentation, but it continues though any number of these prove false. Beliefs as to its nature are essential. Only by and through them can we ever hope to discover modes of life calculated to release the value–potential in the universe. Tentativeness characterizes beliefs; certainty characterizes the attitude. If we forget tentativeness, beliefs ossify and become vicious. If we forget certainty, the very necessity of beliefs vanishes and the acids of cynicism begin their work.

VIII

SYNTHESIS OF TENTATIVENESS
AND CERTAINTY IN CHRISTIAN THEOLOGY

THEOLOGY FACES BOTH TENTATIVENESS
AND CERTAINTY

A BRIEF assessment of the theological implications of the preceding line of thought is perhaps overdue. This, it seems to me, is the heart of the matter: Theology is the discipline above all others which can and should keep tentativeness and certainty in a polar relationship. Which may sound strange to a generation that has seen theology kicked from pillar to post as an impossible attempt to guarantee a short cut to certainty. On the surface, theology's concern is with certainty; she is the acknowledged custodian of religious truths, though now she is usually depicted like Jerusalem of old, " a widow weeping for her children." Granted, immediately, orthodox theology has been preoccupied with dogmas and doctrines whose truths rest ultimately upon revelation. Granted, also, that theology has, in a pinch, favored the deliverances of faith over the conclusions of reason. Granted, finally, that these tactics have led to the breach between theology and the " modern mind."

Granting all this we should, none the less, never permit *credo quia absurdum* to blind us to the basic fact that theology, even in her most autocratic days, insisted upon two significant items. (1) Theology is relevant to life. Its doctrines are worthy of belief because they are true, not in any remote sense but precisely because they are related in a positive way to human problems.[1] The humanity of theology, its serious and sustained endeavor to solve immediate as well as ultimate problems, is a vital characteristic too often overlooked by critics. It is obvious that its method of solving human problems was frequently inadequate, especially when the crucial problems were plagues and famines. Roger Bacon put the case sharply when he opined that the best way to check the typhoid epidemic then raging was to analyze ditch water rather than to say more masses. No sane man would disagree with him; yet it is pertinent to point out that, lacking either the notion or the means of analyzing ditch water, the next best and only thing for a realist to do would be to say mass, because no other method for dealing with the diabolical character of a plague had been devised.

(2) Theology has almost invariably affirmed the ability of reason to discover empirical evidence sufficient to indicate the rationality of dogmas even though their real authorization is by revelation. Many mystics like Bernard of Clairvaux and Meister Eckhart would disagree; even Luther would register a violent protest, though he fell back on Melanchthon's steady reasoning when formulating his theology. But Augustine, Abélard, Aquinas and most other influential thinkers took the position emphasized.

It is my contention that when these two neglected aspects of theology are given sufficient attention, theology will be able to use tentativeness as an attribute of equal importance with certainty. To put the case definitively: Religion is an attempt to keep a system of values in an organic relationship with both the insights and the perplexities of human life. In its endeavor to fulfill this heavy demand religion utilizes three techniques, each of which may be pursued separately,

[1] Cf. W. H. Bernhardt, " A Preface to Theology," *Religion in Life,* I, 358 ff.

yet which it, with prophetic genius, holds together. First, its theology either appropriates or fashions a philosophy of value. This is much more than a plain listing of values (virtues or ends); it consists of a metaphysics and theory of knowledge of values, as well as a method for testing them; without these two there can be no validation of values. Second, religion emphasizes worship as a definite means of deepening reverence for value in general and specific values in particular. Third, every religion ties its theology to life by means of an ethical code — a "this do and thou shalt live" or "one thing thou lackest" — which is both an expression of, and an opportunity to test, the valuational insights gained through thought about and adoration of value.

I readily grant that orthodox theology does not admit that its insights can be empirically disproved and am prepared to insist that any theology which survives contemporary criticism should and must make this admission. In earlier chapters I have tried to indicate reasons why the claims to finality of theological doctrines must be abandoned. If it is admitted that the content and conclusions of religious beliefs can and must be kept sensitive to changing and accumulating experiences, it is inevitable that an ancient test of truth should be embraced: "By their fruits shall ye know them." Let it be noted that whoever in his quest for certainty requires finality of theology must be willing to see it divorced both from specific human problems and from accord with reason. Such a theology would be a compact curio, a marvel of completed perfection, yet quite irrelevant to empirical existence. It is precisely because most of us are not willing to accept this alternative that a new age of theology is upon us. That this is true is evidenced by the amount of attention theological thinkers are giving the three perplexing problems dealt with in this and subsequent chapters: investigation of the implications of current philosophies of value in an endeavor to determine their contribution to the religious approach to human problems; investigation of the meaning of worship, to appraise it as a possible personal and social approach to the universe upon which we are dependent; determination of the ethical implications of philosophies of value. The chief concern of this book is to understand how tentativeness and certainty interact in the various areas. It will be seen that inasmuch as these problem-centers are integral to theology, theology will and does reflect what is found in them.

THE FUNCTIONAL PHILOSOPHY OF VALUE[2]

Lewis says that philosophy is not discovery of novelties but rather a clarification of what already exists in vague and ill defined ways in human experience.[3] Evidence of this is found in philosophies of value. They come into existence in order to describe, analyze and render available for specific predictions a fundamental " consciousness of value." A philosophy of value in order to do this must endeavor to explain the nature of value, how it is known, if it can be known, and to produce a standard or criterion for determining dimensions, proportions or degrees among specific instances. This means that a philosophy of value is an excursion into metaphysics (theory of reality) and epistemology (theory of knowledge); which in turn indicates the fundamental fact that these philosophical areas serve a theory of value much as the broad base of a pyramid serves its apex.

But the point of departure, the *sine qua non* of any and

---

[2] John Dewey and Henry N. Wieman are exponents of this theory; much of the following exposition is drawn from the writings of one or the other or both.

[3] Lewis, *Mind and the World Order*, pp. 2 ff.

every philosophy of value is a consciousness of value. Which is to say that the specific endeavor to state the meaning of truth, beauty, goodness or any other value is, first, to indicate certain types of experience which have been encountered prior to this recognition, and, second, to call attention to their essential quality. Certainty derives both from the consciousness of the reality of such experiences and from confidence in the method of describing, analyzing, and placing them in conceptual form. Tentativeness manifestly derives from the fact that the experiences are items of empirical reality, and judgments placed upon them, purporting to reveal their essential quality, must appeal to future experiences for their substantiation and must, therefore, lay claim to probable rather than certain truth.

All of which may be considerably clarified if we illustrate by a discussion of the functional philosophy of value which impresses me as the most fruitful one up for consideration.

This is to be distinguished, on the one hand, from subjectivism, which equates liking or satisfaction with value, and, on the other, from that form of realism which is so insistent upon the objectivity of values that it is negligent about relating them to human experience. The functional philosophy of value mediates between these extremes, agreeing with the former that value has no meaning when divorced from the experience of enjoyment born of satisfied desires, and with the latter that such enjoyment is dependent in part upon objective factors to which human desires may be adjusted but which are not plastic in any other sense.

The unit of value, the point at which thought on value begins, is an enjoyable situation,[4] which, upon analysis, exhibits three distinct parts: (1) an experiencing mind, (2) an

[4] Wieman's phrase.

experienced object, (3) other factors conditioning the relationship. Although the last is a sort of catchall category, it, along with the first two, deserves closer scrutiny.

(1) The experiencing mind is indispensable to any value. The experiencing mind may be only a possibility, but it can be no less if the situation is to be called a value. Every conscious state has a tinge of liking or disliking, fulfillment or frustration, satisfaction or dissatisfaction. Consciousness as a practical enterprise in the sense of relating things to itself or itself to things is not neutral. It is for or against the situation in which it finds itself, actually or imaginatively. If enjoyment is the clue to value, it follows that an experiencing mind is an indispensable ingredient of value.

Since the experiencing mind is integral to the value situation it exercises a certain measure of control over the situation. This control may take the form of some adjustment. If one is viewing a painting from an angle at which the colors blur, one can move to another point of view which mediates the beauty of the picture. We must neither exaggerate nor minimize the importance of the measure of practical control which the experiencing mind exercises in the value. Man cannot, by fiat, create value; but value cannot exist without man.

The experiencing mind introduces a temporal span into a specific enjoyable situation by adducing a prospective reference. This foresight or adumbration takes the form of meaning. This meaning may or may not be explicitly in consciousness at the moment of experience. A traveler once remarked, " It means a lot to me to have stood on the edge of the Grand Canyon." It is doubtful if the moment of the experience contained a specification of the various ways in which the experience was to influence the future, but that they were genuine possibilities cannot be doubted. The experiencing mind may introduce the prospective reference by way of vivid memory of the situation, which memory will gradually modify one's life, or the impression may be so profound that, in a moment, old standards of meaning are torn down and greater limits within which new ones must be built marked out.[5] In either case, the enjoyable situation is appropriated by the experiencing mind as an open rather than closed event, for meanings stream forth from it conditioning future behavior. The degree of valuehood achieved by an enjoyable situation is determined by the range and intensity of such meanings.

(2) The second component of an enjoyable situation is the experienced object. The factor of objectivity, of "thereness," is an integral part of an enjoyable situation.

An experienced object presents an "aesthetic surface," a pattern of qualities by which it is known. This includes colors, sounds, shapes, with their possibilities of engendering an emotional response. Some objects are superior to others as factors in an enjoyable situation, because the pattern of qualities which they exhibit displays four characteristics in a superior measure: (1) richness — by which is meant the number and diversity of qualities; (2) clarity — which denotes that the pattern can be easily distinguished and perceived; (3) unity — the qualities actually comprise a pattern which is one aesthetic surface of the object; (4) vividness — which is a correlate of the preceding characteristics, and designates the uniqueness of the particular pattern of qualities by which immediate and compelling recognition is given.

[5] Cf. William P. Montague's autobiographical essay in *Contemporary American Philosophy*, George P. Adams and William P. Montague, eds. (The Macmillan Co., 1930), for a vivid example of the way in which old standards are swept away by the torrent of inarticulate meanings engendered by a form of mystic experience.

In addition to the pattern of qualities which the experienced object exhibits there are certain practical requirements which likewise characterize it. If control of an enjoyable situation is possible in any degree, it is because the experienced object has features which permit this control. This aspect of the object may be designated as its structure as distinct from its aesthetic surface. The structure of a great painting is painfully obvious to the amateur who endeavors to copy it. Not only do the brilliance and blend of colors drive him to despair, but the proportions of parts and whole alike of the canvas, without which the aesthetic surface could not exist, also baffle him. Every great artist paints into his pictures a philosophy of structure or proportion which is an organic aspect of his creations. To enter into an enjoyable situation in which a great painting is the experienced object does not mean that one must endeavor to copy it. But the various perspectives of the canvas which comprise its totality are determined by the structure of the painting. Knowledge of the fact that a particular picture is at its best when viewed from a certain angle is recognition of the structure which obtains in it together with directions as to the most satisfactory form of adjustment.

A very important feature of the experienced object is its connection with other actual or possible enjoyable situations. Earlier we referred to the man who had been profoundly impressed by the Grand Canyon. The experienced object was the indescribable beauty and grandeur of the canyon. Yet this canyon has definite connections with other enjoyable situations. That it has such is owing to the meaning it had for the beholder. Though he was unable to articulate the precise form of the meanings it is evident that because of them he felt himself to be a different man. One significant specifiable change is this: he was more receptive to beauty. Hence wherever or whenever he comes into the presence of beauty, whatever its locus, the Grand Canyon is an operative factor. For him, the Grand Canyon as the experienced object in an enjoyable situation was of immeasurable worth because it had lifted his aesthetic consciousness to new levels of sensitivity.

(3) The third component of an enjoyable situation is plural in number rather than singular. It is composed of what may be called, for lack of a more specific term, outside factors. This refers to factors outside consciousness, objective to it as well as to the experienced object. One such is the cultural background of the experiencing individual. It may be asserted that the cultural background is within the experiencing mind. To a large extent this is true, but it can hardly be argued that the cultural background is exhausted by its influence on the mind. It is an objectively real factor to both the experiencing mind and the experienced object, though it may be influential in the formation of both. It furnishes an atmosphere, so to speak, within which the experiencing mind and the experienced object unite. It determines the character of the world; for example, the books, magazines and art forms within which the meanings discovered in a value situation must grow and develop.

Another outside factor is the presence of certain pervasive natural structures which are indispensable to the situation. We refer to certain orders of nature, for one thing. If the enjoyable situation has as its object a beautiful landscape, the orders of nature designated would be the condition of the sky, the angle of the sun, the quality of the atmosphere. Reverting to our friend viewing the Grand Canyon, it is conceivable that the day might have been such that the scene would have made a totally different impression upon him. Rain, wind, sandstorm, etc. — any one of these would have or might have actually altered the entire meaning of the situation.

Although the enjoyable situation may be thus analyzed into various factors, one fact keeps forcing itself upon us as we consider each factor, namely, that the enjoyable situation is an actual, vital organic unity. The slightest alteration in any factor issues in a new situation. Each part supports, modifies, enhances, hence means, every other part.

An enjoyable situation may have any degree of inclusiveness. In fact, inclusiveness is the standard by which the value of an enjoyable situation is judged. If the factors are of such a nature that their meaning implies a great system of other enjoyable situations, the situation is of great value.

The problem of life is how to connect enjoyable situations until they form an inclusive system. Every significant quest in life is for the important meanings of an enjoyable situation in order that it may be vitally related to the other great meanings by which life exists. Yet it is important to remember the fact that every enjoyable situation which comes to be a value is never completely exhausted by any moment of existence. Its prospective reference, its meanings, constitute a cloud of possibilities, some few of which are shed at any given time. The common lament, " If only I had known! " illustrates the point. For it admits with poignant simplicity that some antecedent situation had a multiplicity of meanings which either were not known or were passed over lightly. The ones that were selected as significant did not fulfill their high promise. Hence the longing for another chance to ally oneself with different meanings in the past situation.

There is something unique about every enjoyable situation. Its uniqueness naturally cannot be reproduced, but its dominant meanings are as a rule sharable. Art and literature are set to the task of singling out and dramatizing such meanings. The tremendous influence of religion is attributable to the flood of meaning, derived from previous value situations, which it pours into present perplexities. We shall see in later chapters how the central symbols of the Christian religion have grown more valuable through the ages by gathering into themselves the profound experiences of succeeding generations. Nowhere does the genius of the Christian religion display itself to better advantage than in its dealings with defeats and tragedies, for it raises them to the status of significant values. As the initial step, it insists that they are not ultimate: " Weeping may endure for a night, but joy cometh in the morning " — the source of this confidence being God who is able to provide, and that abundantly, for the needs of his children. Then as a fitting symbol of this stupendous faith the crucifixion and death of Jesus are inseparably linked with his resurrection and ascension. Hence Christians speak of the day when he was crucified and died as " Good Friday," because it issues in the triumphant celebration of Easter morning.

The theological implications of the preceding analysis of the unit of value will become apparent when we center attention upon its metaphysical and epistemological implications.

One prime metaphysical consideration is this: Values are organic to nature and are neither superimposed upon it nor achieved in spite of it. This is not tantamount to saying that nature has as its sole concern the creation and promotion of values. It is simply to affirm that whenever and wherever values occur they are identifiable relationships in nature. The activities which underlie all values are types of interaction between forms of nature. Take the value of health for example. It is the organic result of a number of activities such as breathing, eating, drinking, sleeping, exercising, playing and working. These unite in one organism to produce health. For man, at least, this value does not exist in haughty isolation. Rather it tends to fuse with other values, such as education, culture, economic security, social status, creative work, to produce the abundant life. My present point is that anywhere you touch the structure of values, whether the unit or the largest aggregate of units known to man, it is part and parcel of nature.

All of which can be summarized by the statement that man is an integral part of nature. He not only discovers relations among objects and processes in nature outside himself, but he is related to them as much as they are to one another. Even the fact of discovery simply intensifies the interrelation of natural objects. When man discovers something about himself, such as the circulation of the blood or the process by which he has developed, he augments his knowledge of nature. "Nature's place in man," writes Dewey, "is no less significant than man's place in nature. Man in nature is man subjected; nature in man, recognized and used, is intelligence and art . . . the fact of integration in life is basic." [6] Man as a phase of nature sustains observable relations with other phases. But livelihood and security have always aimed at a much closer integration with the phases that sustain and promote life than man has yet been able to obtain. He must therefore manipulate nature, himself included, until the sense of frustration and hazard is removed or at least minimized.[7]

[6] *Experience and Nature*, p. 28.

[7] Walter Lippmann indicates that our only hope lies in scaling down our demands until they are satisfied by the meager offerings of nature.

The fact of intelligence gives man a strategic position in nature largely because through it the scope of actual or potential relationships is increased to include portions of past, present and future.

A reasonably exact functional description of mind is that it is the capacity for doing three things at once: (1) manipulating the present circumstances (2) by skills born of past experience (3) toward the achievement or in the direction of future ends. Certainly reflection enables man to treasure up his significant hopes and dreams until in some way he can incorporate them in existence. As long as man recognizes himself as that part of nature which is capable of some degree of self-direction and manipulation of his environment, his cause in the cosmos is not hopeless. Puny and weak though he may be when laid alongside the universe, he does not find the universe indifferent to his efforts to manipulate it. The universe does not coddle man as an only-begotten son, yet it manifests approachability. Consider Dewey's conviction that " nature . . . is idealizable. It lends itself to operations by which it is perfected. The process is not a passive one. Rather nature gives, not always freely, but in response to search, means and material by which the values we judge to have supreme quality may be embodied in existence. It depends upon the choice of man whether he employs what nature provides and for what ends he uses it." [8]

Another significant metaphysical inference from the preceding analysis is that values are dynamic aspects of reality. We have seen how the value " health " is an organic unity of discrete activities and how the abundant life is the most inclusive unity of the great values that are open to man. It is,

[8] *The Quest for Certainty*, p. 302. Cf. also E. S. Ames, *Religion* (New York: Henry Holt & Co., 1929).

therefore, characteristic of values that they tend to lose (integrate) themselves in larger unities. Only those enjoyments which can so integrate themselves possess potential value.

A third inference is reached by adding the first two together; namely, the criterion of value is this: Greatest value is to be found in the most inclusive system of mutually sustaining and meaningful enjoyable situations.[9] This is the yardstick for determining whether an enjoyment is an apt candidate for valuehood, or which of two values is the more significant.

The epistemological implications of this philosophy of value are equally significant. Knowledge of value is empirical since values are specific relationships in nature and must therefore be approached like any other form of empirical knowledge.[10] There are three definite component parts in knowledge of value which deserve separate statement although they are fused into a vital unity in life: (1) the experience of enjoyment; (2) the judgment of value; (3) verification via consequences which confirm the judgment.

The fact of experienced enjoyment is the given [11] of knowledge of value. It is the clue to the possible immanence of a certain relationship in nature. Man, as one element in the relationship, approaches the given with a consciousness of value born of past experiences. He adjudges the present enjoyment a value of some degree or other, depending upon his conception of its ability to integrate itself with his value system. In this his guiding light is intelligence, which proceeds upon the information garnered by past experience and made

---

[9] This is what Wieman means by supreme value and God. Cf. his paper, "God and Value," in *Religious Realism,* edited by D. C. Macintosh (New York: The Macmillan Co., 1931), pp. 155–56.

[10] Chap. V contains an analysis of the structure of empirical knowledge.

[11] Cf. Chap. V.

available for rapid judgment in the form of beliefs or hypotheses which embody the implications of the funded wisdom. This equipment for value judgments exists prior to any conscious use of it in measuring an enjoyment.[12] And the whole thrust of the judgment is into the unknown future. It is a statement of what will come to pass but its truth or falsity is determined by the accuracy with which it has predicted the consequences which actually do eventuate from the enjoyment. Esau enjoyed the mess of pottage; Jacob went hungry, apparently, but enjoyed Esau's meal even more than Esau did. Each had made a value judgment relative to an enjoyment and one was grievously disappointed when some consequences which he had chosen to ignore as possibilities actually came to pass. Esau's judgment of value was contradicted by further experience. The pottage doubtless contributed to his momentary health and therefore to his happiness, but when it ceased contributing to his health, his happiness was negated by other consequences overlooked by his judgment of value.

Not all cases of value judgment are as manifestly simple as this one. But the principle is valid throughout life. Expert advice is valuable because it is supposed to take into account possible consequences not apparent to the lay mind. Religion has made abundant use of it. The prophets of Israel surveyed their day and offered counsel based upon value judgments. Certain great ethical generalizations are simply articulations of the totality of the prophetic belief about value: " Sin brings punishment," or " The soul that sinneth, it shall die." Each of these was capable of application to specific instances of sin. Whether this proved a valid application de-

---

[12] This is not to say that it is an inherited quantity. Rather we have every reason to believe that it is the human organism's way of reacting to environment.

pended upon the consequences which actually came to pass, and this lay with the future. This was so patently true to experience that both Jeremiah and the prophetic writers of Deuteronomy stated that the only way to determine whether a prophet is a true or false one is to wait and see how accurate his predictions are. " By their fruits ye shall know them " speaks for itself on the adequate criterion of truth in life.

SOME THEOLOGICAL IMPLICATIONS
OF THIS PHILOSOPHY OF VALUE

The theological implications of the functional philosophy of value are profoundly related to many if not most of the crucial doctrines of traditional Christian thought. While there is good authority for not trying to pour new wine into old wineskins, we have just seen that the idea is scarcely new wine since the prophets and Jesus used it. A casual acquaintance with Christian thought is sufficient to indicate that it is a wholly false metaphor to liken theological doctrines to wineskins. As Shailer Mathews and S. J. Case have pointed out, doctrines are always organic aspects of social life and derive their vitality from that relationship.[13]

1. The Doctrine of God. It is a flat contradiction of fact to assert that the Christian tradition stands squarely behind some one conception of God. That tradition has always supported a vigorous doctrine of God but interpretations of the precise meaning of the doctrine have been multiple and prolific. It is impossible to get unanimity among the acknowledged intellectual giants of the Christian tradition. Origen, Augustine, Erigena, Aquinas, Luther and Calvin,

---

[13] Mathews, *The Growth of the Idea of God, The Atonement and the Social Process;* Case, *Jesus Through the Centuries* (Chicago: University of Chicago Press, 1932), *Highways of Christian Doctrine* (Chicago: Willett, Clark & Co., 1936).

when studied on this subject present interesting and fundamental differences of opinion. Nor were these divergences
solely within the ranks of the thinkers; the perennial feud between the rationalists and the mystics (sometimes within the
same person as in Augustine) always flared up on the subject
of the nature of God. Although the theology of the church
from Aquinas onward has insisted upon the rationality of
the doctrine, which in turn implies the applicability of such
attributes as good, etc., a profound tendency in mysticism has
insisted that God is beyond the reach of predicates of any
kind.[14] The large number of heretical movements and figures (many of them deriving from controversy over the idea
of God) which appear on every page of Christian history
testify both to the constant effort on the part of the church
to secure unanimity and to her inability to do so.

Yet almost all the endeavors to state the meaning of the
doctrine of God in concrete terms have utilized certain
concepts which did help. All agree that God is Creator.
Whether of everything, including the devil, is a moot question, but the salient fact is that God is a creative spirit and is
perpetually present in and among his creatures, which include the subhuman levels of existence as well as the human
levels.

Also, the adjectives " immanent " and " transcendent " appear with practical unanimity. They indicate the fact that
God is both within and beyond the world. As Creator he is
involved in it not alone in the act of creation but also as its
continuing strata of laws. But he is not contained by the
world. He transcends it spatially because he is the totality of
Being within which the world occurs. He transcends it temporally because his Being is the eternality within which its

[14] Dionysius the Areopagite and St. John of the Cross exemplify this tendency.

changes occur. He transcends it as cause transcends effect, as the law of change transcends changes.

Perhaps the most significant quartet of phrases traditionally used is: the will of God, the justice of God, the grace of God, and the love of God. These are significant because all relate God to the ever present facts of ethical choice, struggle, failure and success.

The will of God denotes the law of God's being which is relevant to each and every choice which confronts all men everywhere. There is a right and a wrong way to choose and the decisive factor is the will of God; it is the right way. The obvious fact that we are not able clearly to discern the will of God is better explained by our finitude than by his inconstancy or irrelevance. Either the church (for the Catholic tradition) or the Bible (for the Protestants) was supposed to be able to furnish light on the fuller nature of the will of God in order to facilitate wise choices.

The justice of God, taken by itself or accepted as the dominant attribute of God (as Calvin did), yields a universe of inexorable moral law. God is constant goodness and he requires that his creatures conform to the laws of his being. The reward of obedience is salvation; that is, eternal happiness. The punishment for failure to conform, *regardless of the cause,* is swift and awful. " Be not deceived, God is not mocked," might well be inscribed over the Christian doctrine of God. It is the negative rendering of a positive point, namely, that God has a definite nature the laws of which are the laws of existence.

The grace of God prevents the justice of God from being simply a universal moral law such as that basic in Buddhism. But grace denotes worlds more than mere kindness and benevolent sympathy. It is God searching for man in order to redeem him. Man, through either original sin or choice, suffers because he has failed to conform to the will of God. The grace of God is tenderly symbolized in the parable of the Lost Sheep; it is God who by searching him out brings man into renewed contact with Himself, thereby making salvation possible.

The love of God is the most inclusive of the phrases. It gathers the will, the justice and the grace of God into itself and fuses them into a warm affectional unity: God loves man. Jesus is the constant symbol of this love. His sacrifice, symbolized by every cross in Christendom, is eloquent testimony to the real depths of God's love. This love is not passing fancy; it is God in his totality. It does not negate his justice nor does it soften his will — these are integral to his being — but the love of God describes the whole of which these are parts. Another way of describing it is to say that God's share in the redemption of man is out of all proportion to all the repenting and efforts at goodness which men may do and make. How else is it possible that " the just shall live by faith "? Luther's discernment of this truth — it is at least as old as the character of the Father in Jesus' parable of the Prodigal Son — gave him a peace which all his efforts at penance could not bring.

These, then, are some of the widely used ways in which the doctrine of God was explained and related to human problems. Attention has been called to them because they illustrate the relationship between the functional philosophy of value and Christian theology.

It is important at this juncture to reaffirm the fact that it is the purpose of theology to relate a philosophy of value to recurrent human problems. There is some philosophy of value embedded in every theology and any philosophy of value has implications for human problems. Whether the implications are numerous and profound enough to minister to the range of need is an important question. Theology can make little or no use of a philosophy of value that is wholly subjective, where value is tantamount to liking or satisfied desire. Neither can it render religiously significant one that divorces the essential existence of value from the scene of human choices, making of value a perfect entity which hovers over existence, giving the illusion of relevance yet being wholly self-contained. In addition, theology cannot put to any enduring use a philosophy of value that does not proclaim the reality of a value hierarchy; it must be possible to grade, rank and systematize concrete values.

Lest the preceding remarks sound like prompting reality on her lines, a laying down of the law to the universe, so to speak, as to what it must be like, let me say that the only inference to be drawn is that if theology cannot find a philosophy of value which is both relevant to human problems and yet objective to them, which, in addition, points out a gradation of values, then theology has fallen on evil days. And that is precisely what has happened historically. The Renaissance was a fundamental revolution in philosophy of value. Since the breakup of the medieval synthesis no philosophy of value has been able to reorder the resulting confusion. Theology has been on the skids since that epoch. It has been in constant turmoil, trusting its case first to the subjectivistic value theory of romanticism, and then to the realistic value theory implied by the doctrine of universal law in rationalism. With the challenging of each of these theology has been challenged. Today it is endeavoring to fulfill its ancient obligation, that is, meeting human needs by means of various value theories. Hence this attempt to see what lies ahead for theology in the functional philosophy of value.

What does the doctrine of God mean in terms of this philosophy of value?[15] Let it be noted at once that God is supreme value. He is not the sensation of pleasure which characterizes every enjoyment but he is that integrative aspect of an enjoyment through which it merges with other enjoyments to form a system, thereby becoming a value. A value is a fact; that is, it has a definite structure by virtue of which it is recognized and known. Plato would say that a value has an " essence "; Aristotle would call it a " form "; Whitehead would call it a " structure "; but all agree that it is the distinguishing thing about a value. Now this essence, form or structure of a value is its integrative potential. When an enjoyment manifests this characteristic, it is a value.[16] When one value displays a greater potentiality than another, it is a greater value. Why should this be so? Is it not because of the very nature of value itself, which is integration? That distinguishing characteristic by virtue of which value is value must be regarded as supreme value. And this theology can confidently and with clear conscience denote as God, because that concept has always been used to symbolize the basic value structure of mankind.

The traditional attribute of Creator fits in with the notion that fundamentally God is supreme value. There is definite ground for asserting that God so conceived is the most potent force or aspect of existence. Scientific theories of development, based upon the accumulating research of two centuries, testify to the fact that there is evidence of a tendency of progressive integration in existence. God might be defined as that aspect of progressive integration in the universe which

---

[15] Here I acknowledge my heavy indebtedness to Professor Wieman, most of whose published works have been devoted to answering this question.

[16] Thomas Aquinas insists upon the "connectedness of virtues" (*Summa Theologica*, VIII, 173 ff.).

manifests itself on the human level in the growth of values. This does not assert that the universe throughout is God-controlled. As Borden Parker Bowne once said to his students, " there is such a thing as getting too much God in the world." But there is good warrant for asserting that there is a discernible drift of direction in cosmic processes.[17] A brief survey of the factual basis of this statement is in order.

The exact sciences tell a story which, though incomplete in detail, is precise in outline and is probably familiar even to laymen. The ultimate unit of existence, whether energy or matter or both, is what it is because of its interrelationships. Electrons and protons unite to form atoms; atoms to form molecules; molecules, cells; cells, tissues; tissues, organs; organs, organisms. Here the social sciences take up the task and point out that organisms coalesce to produce societies of a graduating complexity. Man, the unit of society, is borne up by an ocean of interrelationships, physical and social alike. His health and happiness depend upon the establishment and maintenance of a stable, dynamic pattern of interaction called " growth " in which customs, ideas, inventions, religions and philosophies of all kinds are conditioning factors much as various brooks and streams pool their flow in a river.

Nor does science stand alone in this conception of a directional thrust in the universe. Modern philosophy, in the persons of S. Alexander, A. N. Whitehead, C. Lloyd Morgan, R. W. Sellars, Nicolai Hartmann, Henri Bergson and, to some extent, John Dewey, has been working out the broader philosophic implications of the position and has produced some profound results. It is safe to say that since the publication of Darwin's *Origin of Species* in 1859 every great phi-

17 I have developed this notion in some detail in " Wanted: An Absolute," *Christian Century,* Dec. 2, 1936, pp. 1606–9.

losopher of the Western world has accepted some form of directional development as an ultimate fact.

Thus we see that the notion of integration as the distinguishing mark of value is in reality the distinguishing mark of a cosmic process which reaches down to the very elements of existence and streams up to man, supporting his entire being, and beyond him in the form of possibilities of greater values, some of which find expression in his dreams and ideals, others of which are doubtless unrecognized. The essence of creativity is the combination of existing materials in new patterns with the occasional result of discovering a new structure with an integrity of its own. Nor need this be left in the realm of abstraction. Friendship is an example of creativity as truly as is the union of atoms of hydrogen and oxygen to produce a molecule of water. Social psychology is supplying us with abundant evidence that selves are social creations and actually exhibit new characteristics when placed in new situations.[18]

God so conceived is both immanent and transcendent. As the dynamic ground of creativity and emergence throughout existence he is immanent. He is Creator not only in the specific sense of producing new structures such as life from matter; but he invests with himself, as laws, the very nature of the actual or created continuum.[19] God as the law or foundation of value is, by definition, immanent in even the humblest values. Wherever there are values like health, harmony, understanding, loyalty, friendship, justice, love, there is God.

[18] C. H. Cooley, *Human Nature and Social Organization* (New York: Charles Scribner's Sons, 1902); G. H. Mead, *The Philosophy of the Act* (Chicago: University of Chicago Press, 1938); C. W. Morris, *Six Theories of Mind* (Chicago: University of Chicago Press, 1932); the writings of Dr. Ellsworth Faris.

[19] This is a fundamental notion in S. Alexander's distinction between "deity" and "divine."

But to say that God is immanent in values is not to limit him to coexistence with all actual values. He is transcendent not only as creator of any experienced value but broods over or stretches beyond that value in the form of inherent possibilities. This is what Wieman has in mind when he defines God as that structure of existence and *possibility* which sustains and promotes greatest value.[20] All actual values are confronted by the fact of their incompleteness, their failure really to enter into the most profound kind of organic relationship with other values. Family love is a towering value, yet even it can be prevented from a full realization of its possibilities by the shortsighted parental policy of trying to treat the growing children as if they were babies, or by the equally shortsighted policy of setting family welfare above that of all other persons. In either case the radiance of the value is dimmed; its outpouring in the larger communal life is choked up if not off. God is immanent in family love to the full reach of its valuehood; he transcends it in the form of unrealized possibilities. His transcendence of all actual values can be summarized this way: God is the permanent possibility of greater value. Let us remember that, as such, he does not extend beyond existence as an attenuated something, a pale wraith, a feeble testimony to our incompleteness, nor even as a projection of thwarted desires, but rather he is actual possibility, that is, he has definite structure which can be and is incorporated in actual values in proportion as they realize the possibilities inherent in them as participants in the inclusive system of value.

As we turn to the four phrases which linked the traditional doctrine of God to the problems of human life and endeavor to determine what they mean in terms of the functional phi-

---

[20] *The Wrestle of Religion with Truth* (New York: The Macmillan Co., 1927); *Issues of Life* (New York: Abingdon Press, 1930); and other writings.

losophy of value we might expect that they should lose some of their warmth. True enough, so long as God was regarded as celestial emperor, king or judge, all his attributes were patterned along the lines of human attributes. That this making of God in man's image made God vitally, not to mention ominously, personal need not be denied. But there are other and more meaningful ways in which man's dependence upon God and God's profound meaning for human life can be warmly and richly symbolized. And, at least as I understand them, the traditional phrases — the will, justice, grace and love of God — are adequate and appropriate symbols of these meanings.

The will of God denotes the structure of value wherever and whenever found. It indicates not only the factual nature of actual values but the real structure of their possibilities. Health, friendship, love, the welfare of a society are definite values because they have definite structures. Laws underlie them all. We cannot dictate the nature of any of them. We can only discover it in degree and adjust ourselves to it. We will have hypotheses or beliefs as to what this basic structure is and follow their leading, but reality as encountered in the life process speaks the last word; it pronounces judgments both on our beliefs and on our living. There is then ample evidence in the realm of value for asserting that value structure, supreme value, has a precise character, both relevant to our experience and choices, yet objective to us; which is the fundamental meaning of the " will of God." [21]

The justice of God is shorn of both the caprice and the revenge which too often characterized its meaning in tradi-

---

[21] " The purpose of God is the attainment of value in the temporal world." — Whitehead, *Religion in the Making* (New York: The Macmillan Co., 1926), p. 100.

tional theology.   It calls attention to the fact that since God is the nature of value, whosoever would experience greater value must search for and adjust himself to God.   There will not be, as there have not been, wanting those who will try to legislate regarding the meaning and character of value. Whoever does this will learn that an ancient warning was based upon experience: " It is a fearful thing to fall into the hands of the living God."   After due allowance has been made for the symbolical character of the language, the stubborn, irreducible fact remains that we cannot dictate our own terms of life unless we want to take our exit in one glorious orgy of adolescent self-exhibitionism.   We can have friends, experience love and brotherhood only when we humbly acknowledge the fact that the real meaning of these can be discovered in no other way than that of patient, and perhaps painful, searching.   If we take some great ideal value like brotherhood of man or peace, it is at once obvious that we cannot actualize it either by simply desiring it or by inventing a panacea that glosses over relevant facts.   If either value is achieved, attitudes toward persons and property must be changed until they tend to unify rather than divide mankind. This would require a re-education of most of us along very concrete lines and in terms of daily realities.   I am trying to point out that any value whether great or small has an order or structure in its own being, and one who experiences it does so by conforming to that discovered character.

The grace of God finds pungent expression in the dynamic nature of value.   Not only is there evidence of development in biological species, but the fact of growth is discernible in the values of life.   John Dewey, who cannot be accused of religious bias yet whose thought is logically related to all that has been said about the functional philosophy of value, insists that there is such a thing as the growth of good. "A good is a good anyhow, but to reflection those goods approve themselves, whether labeled beauty or truth or righteousness, which steady, vitalize and expand judgments in creation of new goods and conservation of old goods." [22] Although Dewey keeps goods pluralized, I submit that this statement is fundamentally a plain avowal of the existence of a system of goods which is dynamic and progressive. Any structure of things or goods that conserves the old while steadily increasing it by the addition of the new can correctly be called a dynamic system. Wieman makes a cardinal assertion of the growth of good. He addresses himself to the task of describing the process of progressive integration which is operative on the human level in the form of shared values, and which, as possibilities, stretches out into the unknown and unimaginable future. This process issues in a growth of good in so far as man makes satisfactory adjustment to it. Wieman describes both the nature and the grace of God when he writes: ". . . there is operative in our midst a power which makes for the greatest good by way of increasing our oneness, which way, however, is not our way, for we sin against it, struggle against it, and must find it out by experiment. This increasing oneness that makes for the greatest good is not our work, but we cannot rise to greater good in any other way save by it. This power is sovereign over us in the sense that we must meet the conditions which it imposes or else suffer disaster." [23]

In this connection it may be worth while to draw a distinction between types of interdependence and the growth of good. Interdependence is not necessarily a good. It may be like the wolf's teeth — "The better to eat you with, my

---

[22] *Experience and Nature*, p. 417.
[23] *Is There a God?* p. 163; cf. also p. 124.

dear." The profound interdependence among the nations of this modern world causes very little rejoicing these days. It reminds one of the method of dueling formerly used by certain American Indians. The antagonists had their left arms securely bound together and knives placed in their free hands. They fought until one was dead. Frequently both were killed. The other type of interrelatedness is the growth of good embodied in the principle of love. Its genius lies in this: it is a sharing of the best that one has and finds without thought of restraint or reward, and a continual refining in the fires of life of what one thinks best.

There is nothing inevitable about the growth of good. It does not force itself upon man. Its growth depends upon the willingness and wisdom which man exhibits in his endeavor to cause the increasing interdependence among men to promote rather than destroy the actualities and potentialities of existing values. But the important point relevant to the grace of God is that he stands ready and willing to assist man in this endeavor. But man must realize that " the chief end of man is to glorify God and enjoy him forever " before the resources of God become, to some degree, available.

The love of God — his goodness yearning for man and striving to infuse man with itself — receives powerful justification in the philosophy of value under consideration. God is as real as health, as integral to life as society, as steadfast as deathless loyalties, as warmly radiant as friendship and love. These and all other values known to man are expressions of God in life. But there is much in life that is not value, is even violently hostile to value, such as disease, pain, ignorance, and the divisive attitude and practice of selfishness whether by individuals or groups. When God encounters these, the vivid words of the Psalmist leap to mind: " Our God is a living fire." The struggle between supreme value and disvalue, both as positive evil and as arrested values, is on and ceases only when the loyalty and devotion of the whole personality is given to God or supreme value. Nor should this fact occasion surprise. It flows from the notion that values grow by integrating themselves with other values.

This passionate cohesion among values is the rational basis of the Christian's insistence that God is love. For Jesus, it was unthinkable that one who was not at peace with his brother could worship God. He would not permit men to put the values of life in separate pigeonholes for the simple reason that the good, the abundant life requires recognition of, loyalty to, and exemplification of their organic character.

Supreme value (God) is not a passive mountainside up which men climb. Rather it is encountered in the fleeting experience of some value and the uncontrollable desire for more; it is the portions of truth, beauty and goodness that we know yearning for full realization of themselves; it is the accidental or incidental act of kindness and compassion pleading for the status of enduring habit, or, better still, sensitive custom. God is within, yet beyond, life. He is both the meaning of righteousness and the power which makes for righteousness. He is not all of life but his nature determines the direction in which men move who aspire to the abundant life.

2. *The Doctrine of Salvation.* The logical structure of the doctrine of salvation can be described rather simply. On the one hand, there is the sinfulness of man, on the other, the perfect goodness of God. These are both contradictory and universal; that is, man and sin are coextensive; so also God and perfect goodness. There is a single bridge spanning this otherwise unbridged and unbridgeable gulf. It is the love of

God revealed in the person of Christ through whom it is possible for man to be redeemed from sin. Man must choose God in Christ if he would be saved. Salvation, then, denotes deliverance from the state of sinfulness.

Christian theologians have argued loud and long — suspiciously like the six blind men of Hindustan — about the details of the doctrine. Augustine believed that the action in the process of salvation is wholly from God to man. Man by an act of faith can believe in and appropriate to himself the immeasurable grace of God. Luther, Calvin and the Barthian theologians follow Augustine on this point. John Wesley, following Arminius, a Dutch theologian, developed the notion that perfection is possible to man, and even to this day aspirants to the ministry of the church he founded are asked the staggering question, " Are you going on to perfection? " Important as such details have been historically, we shall not spend time with them. The central notion is that salvation, meaning deliverance from sinfulness, can secure genuine support from the functional philosophy of value.

First, of course, it is important to determine what sinfulness means in terms of the new setting. Three separate though not unrelated answers can be given: (1) Sinfulness means inconstant loyalty to supreme value, (2) insubordinate loyalties, or (3) refusal to recognize and abide by the implications for life of the organic structure of value.

Examples of these have been cited in the preceding section. Others equally pertinent and universal can be sketched. One of the most widespread forms of sinfulness today is that type of patriotism which gives supreme loyalty to country. It is a sin to award supreme loyalty to any institution, whether family, church or state. Loyalty to supreme value does not turn one away from loyalty to these, providing they are regarded

as parts of a larger whole, as organs in an organism of value.
That there is real difficulty in keeping institutional loyalties
from claiming the toga of supreme loyalty is patent to all.
Whether it is hopeless, an "impossible possibility," to use
Reinhold Niebuhr's phrase, is another question. Certain it is
that the logic of institutionalism [24] is the constant foe of value
growth. By logic of institutionalism I mean the tendency of
any institution to "set," to ossify, to "coralize" and form a
rigid reef. To alter the figure, an institution, like an object
in motion or at rest, is governed by a law of inertia which dictates that this mode of behavior shall continue. When the
logic of institutionalism dominates an institution it loses the
capacity of self-criticism. It creates "safe" men and places
them in positions of leadership. It moves by momentum
rather than acceleration; it coasts, but cannot pick up speed.
But when the needs which brought the institution into existence change through growth or other alteration, the logic
of institutionalism puts on a splendid exemplification of what
our pious ancestors meant by personal devil. It lashes out
with epithets and personal recriminations at all who suggest
that it does not meet existing needs. It deprecates the integrity of the critic. It scoffs at the possibility that he is making
his suggestion in good faith as one who honestly believes that
the institution can be modified to meet the needs. Tolerance
dies of strangulation when an established institution is challenged as to its efficiency. The powers that be decree a state
of martial law in the realm of the spirit and are ready to throw
into concentration camps all who do not acquiesce in every
detail to the dictates of the institution.

Yet institutions are essential to the growth of value. In no

[24] Paul Tillich and others use the vivid concept "demonic" to denote the
same phenomenon.

other way can the social nature of the self discover, cultivate and use its capacities. The meaning of value, greater value or supreme value cannot be related to human life except through those activities in and through which life grows. Family, school, church, community, nation, world — there can be no growth of value for man except in terms of some such social organizations. But these organizations are not amorphous masses. They have, must have, determinate structures exhibited in historical antecedents, in laws, rights, obligations, rewards and punishments. But when these determinate structures become *deterministic,* become ends in themselves, then the negation of value begins. Plainly, then, sinfulness does not derive from membership in social organizations, but it is the only adequate way to describe loyalty to an institution which strives to be an end in itself. Obviously the same reasoning applies to a person who regards himself as the sole end of his striving. In other words, sinfulness upon examination turns out to be a distorted interpretation of health, friendship, loyalty, love, etc., which in their pure form are true values.

Salvation, for the functional philosophy of value, continues to denote deliverance from sinfulness. That man is saved who both sees supreme value (the perfect goodness of God) in and beyond existence and dedicates himself to its totality. He is on the road toward salvation whose first step in resolving a choice is sincerely to raise the question: In what direction lies supreme value? "Which is the way where light dwelleth?" He is well along the road to the abundant life who realizes that the dynamic nature of the values which warm and enrich his daily living (the love of God) is aiding him out of all proportion to his own efforts.

3. *The Doctrine of Christ.* To be exact, several Christian doctrines deal with the meaning of Christ. But there is a

single point of view implicit in all, namely, that Christ is the revelation of God. The New Testament, of course, is solidly behind this conception. Historians have pointed out the process whereby the Jewish concept "Messiah" came to be equated with the Greek concept "Logos." Although there is a real difference in their original meanings, the fact remains that both denote someone whose close relationship with God makes him the leader, the savior, of men. The great doctrines with christological bearing — trinity, incarnation and person — are later and meticulously precise logical formulations of this same fundamental point. The net result of their collective endeavor is to explain and try to validate the position which the several preceding centuries of Christians had unanimously accorded Jesus. The rhetorical phrases of the Nicean formula, affirming that Jesus was "very God of very God . . . and was made man," are an attempt to render logically explicit his simple statement, "He that hath seen me hath seen the Father." Paul averred, "I can do all things through him that strengtheneth me." Paul's Christology might fairly be stated in two sentences: When we see Christ we see God. When we have faith in Christ we live in Christ and Christ in us. "*Faith* is a spiritual point of contact, a channel through which Christ's spirit flows into us and makes us like him." [25] These and many other sentiments drawn from the New Testament catch and express the belief, common both to all Christians of that day and to the later Christologies, that Jesus is the revelation of God.

The functional philosophy of value can be applied to this doctrine in much the same way as to the two discussed earlier. We may, even must, continue to affirm that Jesus is the clearest revelation of God that we have. Several elements of change are apparent in this wording. For example, whereas all traditional christological doctrines assert the uniqueness of Jesus, this one affirms his supremacy. Classical formulations make redundant use of the notion that he is the one, the only, the ultimate, the final revelation of God. He may be such, but from the perspective of an empirical philosophy of value conclusive evidence will not be available until the last man is dead. But it is possible to make a strong case for the doctrine of Christ as we have stated it. That our evidence is not exhaustive goes without saying. We know all too little about him and much of the source material is hemmed in by puzzling critical questions, but — and this is the significant point — wherever we turn in his life and teachings we experience a fine integrity born of his devotion to an insight into "the meaning of God in human experience."

It seems, to me at least, unnecessary to make more than briefest mention of those battle-scarred doctrines that deal with the physical, psychical and volitional nature of Jesus. That such doctrines were once integral to theology is obvious. That it is possible to validate them either as historical facts or as logically necessary is wholly another problem. So far as the functional philosophy of value is concerned, they simply are unimportant, unless insisted upon, in which case they are likely to become examples of a vicious form of magic. So far as I can see the most that can be said for them is this: *If* Jesus had to be a unique manifestation of God, symbolized in the virgin birth, and *if* his personality had to be a unique synthesis of deity and humanity in order to achieve his profound interpretation of God, then so be it.

Obviously the trouble lies in the "if" clause. Many will agree with Principal Micklem that the doctrines contained in

it are not hypothetical in any sense.[26]   Yet historical validation of them is far from conclusive.   When theologians attempt to transfer these doctrinal assertions from the assump-
tional clause they must keep clearly in mind the fact that
the only justification for the transfer is the logical necessity
of systematic theology.   And it might be well to see with
equal clarity that logical necessity is not necessarily inter-
changeable with historical fact.

Jesus' insight into the nature of God is conveyed both by his
teachings and by his life.   It revolves around a threefold interpretation of love which for him is the mode through which
God expresses himself.   Jesus insisted upon (1) the centrality of love in the universe; (2) the absolute claim of love upon
man; (3) the validation of love in the sphere of action, of
conduct, in experienced consequences of ethical and religious
choices.

The simple faith that " with God all things are possible " [27]
is the doorway through which we enter into Jesus' conception
of God.   His is the prophetic belief that God is the purpose in
all things; that whatever happens is either determined or allowed by God.   God is the actual cause of all good and the
potential master of all evil — and this because he is perfect
goodness and love.   Human concepts of good and evil are
vague attempts to grasp God's nature, but he transcends them:
" for he maketh his sun to rise on the evil and on the good,
and sendeth rain upon the just and the unjust "; [28] also, " if ye,
being evil, know how to give good gifts unto your children,
how much more shall your Father which is in heaven give
good things to them that ask him ? " [29]   Jesus uses some vivid

---

[26] *What Is the Faith?* (Nashville, Tenn.: Cokesbury Press, 1937), Preface.
[27] Matt. 19:26.
[28] Matt. 5:45.   [29] Matt. 7:11.

metaphors to describe the centrality of love in the universe: "Are not five sparrows sold for two farthings? And not one of them is forgotten before God. But even the very hairs of your head are all numbered. Fear not therefore: ye are of more value than many sparrows."[30] "Wherefore, if God so clothe the grass of the field, which today is, and tomorrow is cast into the oven, shall he not much more clothe you, O ye of little faith?"[31]

The immediate implication of this conception of God is that love lays an absolute claim upon man. "Be ye therefore perfect, even as your Father which is in heaven is perfect."[32] And "the great commandment" is, "Thou shalt love the Lord thy God with all thy heart, and with all thy soul, and with all thy mind."[33] To this end man's desires, his will, must be transformed. The motives for action must be scrutinized and relocated in the Kingdom of God which is "within you." They must unite rather than divide. They must serve love rather than hate.

The degree to which man recognizes the claim of love is determined by his conduct. In the tremendous Judgment Day scene sketched in Matthew 25:31–46 the criterion for dividing men is what they have done when confronted by the fact of human need. The only satisfactory testimony to devotion to God is the presence of works of love. That this leads to conflict and sacrifice Jesus knew all too well.[34] But the Kingdom of God is open only to those whose lives are expressions of His love for men. A man at variance with his

[30] Luke 12:6–7.
[31] Matt. 6:30.
[32] Matt. 5:48.
[33] Matt. 22:37.
[34] See "Jesus and the Pharisees," by Gregory Vlastos (*Christendom*, Winter Number, 1936), for a clear, concise presentation of this point.

brother is wasting his sacrifice if he places it on the altar before being reconciled with his brother. The revolutionary
nature of the Kingdom of God is nowhere better portrayed
than as the reversal of the value judgments by which un-
godly living proceeds, for in this kingdom " the last shall be
first," [35] and " whosoever of you will be chiefest, shall be servant of all," [36] and " by this shall all men know that ye are my
disciples, if ye have love one to another." [37] The deeds which
manifest love range all the way from offering a cup of cold
water in the name of a disciple, through laying down one's
life for his friends, to loving enemies. Love means not alone
the absence of resentment; it means also the forgiving love
which does not seek or desire reprisal. This Jesus both taught
and practiced.

For the functional philosophy of value the central fact of
the universe is that of progressive integration because it sustains and promotes greatest value. Jesus, more clearly than
anyone else, apprehended the nature and meaning of the
value structure of the universe. His application of the concept love, inclusive as it is of the related notions of will, justice
and grace, is both our most sensitive and our most accurate
approach to the fact of God in the world. Nowhere else in
the universe has the value structure which is God risen in
such compelling grandeur as in Jesus' life. What he felt and
discerned as fundamental fact he taught as truth to men. His
life and teachings, therefore, are the clearest revelation of
God that we have. Nor is this statement a denial of the
prerogative of his saviorhood, though the traditional pattern
is changed. Men who believe that when they see Jesus they
see God, and who live by this belief, are saved, are related, not
in any magical but in a profoundly religio-ethical sense, to

[35] Matt. 19:30.   [36] Mark 10:44.   [37] John 13:35.

God. He who dwells in Christ and in whom Christ dwells is saved by God in Christ.

But whoever aspires to this salvation must commit himself without reservation to God. He must be willing to accept the Kingdom of God and God's righteousness as of supreme importance. He must eagerly strive to weave all his discrete loyalties into the one supreme loyalty to God. If some loyalties tend to disrupt the pattern, they must be disciplined or discarded. One cannot walk with God in Christ except he bear a cross which would seem to grow heavier rather than lighter the longer he carries it were it not for the simple fact that the sustaining power of God shares with him the burden.

We have repeatedly insisted that value is as value does. Value is an empirical relationship and is, therefore, a continuing one. Any particular judgment of value is validated to the degree that its actional consequences come to pass. Jesus' criterion, "By their fruits ye shall know them," has already been referred to several times. This is his yardstick for measuring the degree to which love has motivated the actions of men. We who wrestle with the multitude of personal problems which tend to decentralize life energies, and with the social problems which split mankind into warring camps, can do no better than to wrestle in his name and for his sake. If, and to the degree that, the supreme loyalty of our lives is to God as revealed in Christ, we shall be able to lay, with peace and confidence, our actions as offerings on his altar.

TENTATIVENESS AND CERTAINTY IN THEOLOGY

Two endeavors have thus far in this chapter occupied our attention: (1) the functional philosophy of value; (2) its implications for theology, stated in terms of both traditional doctrines and present needs. One further task remains, namely, that of determining more exactly those aspects or phases of theological procedure, some of which are properly regarded as sources of certainty and others of tentativeness. Four such are clearly distinguishable. Both logically and chronologically prior to any particular judgment of value is the consciousness of value which has been discussed briefly in the preceding pages. It will be sufficient, at this juncture, simply to say that it denotes our realization that the facts of better and worse stretch out ahead of any and every choice. This realization is a deposit of past experience and the frame of reference which gives credence to any particular judgment of value. It is, then, a priori to the individual judgment and is one of the sources of certainty.[38]

The second phase of the valuational process is that of rendering the consciousness of value rational; that is, of placing it in such form that it can be readily articulated in the form of value judgments. This means an endeavor to determine the nature, meaning and test of value; in other words, its metaphysics and epistemology. The functional philosophy of value which has been occupying our attention is one such endeavor. It presupposes the consciousness of value in life and tries to isolate the essential aspects of value. Manifestly it must be held tentatively, that is, as the best formulation we have, yet answerable for its permanent validity to all future empirical experiences.

The third phase is the judgment of value based upon the philosophy of value which in turn is an articulation of the consciousness of value. The judgment is an endeavor to predict the course of the consequences by bringing the beliefs

[38] Cf. Chap. V.

about value to bear in the act of choosing. It is characterized by tentativeness as is its parent, the philosophy of value.

The concluding phase of the valuational procedure is the method by which the truth of a judgment is determined. Needless to say, the method used is not unrelated to the structure of the philosophy of value. If this, for example, holds that the real locus of value is some type of supernatural reality, it would then be useless to attempt to measure it by an empirical criterion, such as the method of observation and reason. Yet there is no other way of evaluating a judgment which deals with empirical facts. Value theorists must, therefore, choose between two alternatives. Either value is irrelevant to life, in which case value judgments would not be made; or value is a conditioning factor in empirical existence and both explains the presence of the consciousness of value and produces consequences many if not most of which can be observed and related to past and future experiences through value judgments. So far as I know no one has ever chosen the first alternative.

John Oman's supernaturalism locates absolute value in supernatural reality, to be sure, but this continually impregnates nature to produce relative values, which comprise the subject matter of ethics. Although Hartmann, following Plato, conceives values as essences which form a resplendent rainbow over existence, he insists that one ineradicable characteristic of all values is the "ought-to-be" which when apprehended by man translates itself into the "ought-to-do." For both thinkers, then, the method of evaluating value judgments must of necessity be empirical. We have seen how the functional philosophy of value which views value as an integral aspect of existence frankly says that value judgments have to do with relations within nature that are different from other relations only in degree of complexity, rather than in kind, and that, for it, the criterion of all empirical judgments is the only one capable of passing on the validity of value judgments.

There is therefore nothing tentative about the method of observation and reason as the criterion for validating value judgments. It is a source of genuine certainty, not alone because it utilizes the logical structure of " if-then " which underlies logical certitude, but also because it recognizes and deals with values as aspects of nature, of empirical reality, underlying the primal consciousness of value and validating or invalidating judgments of value.

Theology as that aspect of religion which endeavors to relate a philosophy of value to the perplexities and the insights of human life can scarcely avoid accepting the various phases of valuational procedure and the tentativeness and certainty which characterize them. But theology is more than thought about value; it is the attempt to translate such thought into daily living. Therefore " consciousness of value " becomes reverence for value which is the distinguishing characteristic of the religious attitude. A theological system is a comprehensive, coherent and precise attempt to articulate the specific meanings of reverence for value. It utilizes commonly accepted symbols not alone in order to explain the nature of value but especially to convey reverence for value. Hence the value structure of philosophy becomes the Father God of religious devotion; the nature of value becomes the " love that will not let me go "; the hierarchical structure of values becomes the will and purpose of " Him in whom we live and move and have our being." All theological doctrines or religious beliefs, such as those discussed earlier in this chapter, are attempts to focus both reverence for value and concrete ideas about value upon specific areas of human living. For its vitality this enterprise requires that certainty born of reverence for value and tentativeness born of beliefs about its nature and relevance to specific situations be held in a polar relationship. Facts drawn from reflection as well as life warrant both; each without the other becomes meaningless.

Succeeding chapters will deal (1) with the way in which religion endeavors to deepen reverence for value, namely, worship; and (2) with the way it tests the validity of beliefs articulating this reverence, that is, ethical conduct.

IX

SYNTHESIS OF TENTATIVENESS
AND CERTAINTY IN CHRISTIAN WORSHIP

MANY READERS are doubtless prepared to insist that the polarity between tentativeness and certainty, however valuable for theology, breaks down in the area of worship. For them, worship is coextensive with complete conviction. When conviction falters or fails, worship is at an end. Tentativeness in any form, they conclude, destroys the basis of worship. What answer can be made to such an objection?

Of course, its primary weakness is the equation of tentativeness with skepticism. In an earlier section the fallacy of identifying these two was pointed out. Tentativeness and skepticism are different not in degree but in kind; and for several reasons. Whereas skepticism possesses neither point of departure nor sense of direction, tentativeness has both. Skepticism is the rather ungraceful abandonment of the search for truth; tentativeness is the insistent pursuit of truth, albeit sobered by the fact that the future is really unknown and unknowable except as it ceases to be future and becomes present. Skepticism eyes experience and empirical knowledge, sees their weaknesses, irrationalities and fragmentary character, and declines to accept them as safe guides into the surf of breaking presents; tentativeness likewise surveys experience and empirical knowledge, admits that life would be less hazardous if they were more reliable, yet sees in them not only the sole guides we have, but also the guides that can be relied upon (even though their method is essentially that of trial and error) to lead us wherever it is possible for us to go.

Whoever continues to insist that tentativeness so conceived means the death of worship chooses to ignore certain attitudes which have always characterized significant worship. One such is *expectancy:* witness the worry-worn disciples waiting in the upper room before Pentecost; the mystics anxiously, eagerly treading the *via negativa,* leaving behind all deliverances of sense, all judgments, all valuations, even consciousness of self, hoping thereby to find reabsorption into the Whole; the tired farmer, business man or housewife going to church because "sometimes it helps." The worshiper bows humbly, joyfully, reverently before a great and glorious Potency. How it will touch him he does not know. He only knows that he waits before it as a servant awaits the bidding of his master, or better, as a child in need awaits the approach of a loving parent. He who worships listens that he may hear, looks that he may see, feels after something if haply he may touch it, asks that he may receive, seeks that he may find, knocks that it may be opened unto him. He is, in fine, endeavoring to discover and ally himself with the fuller nature of the environing Reality "in whom he lives and moves and has his being."

Groping is another fundamental characteristic of the worshipful attitude. The skeptic cannot worship because he has no sense of direction; neither can one worship whose heart is hardened by the conceit that he is in conscious possession of final truth. The worshiper cries with the troubled soul of an earlier day, "Lord, I believe; help Thou mine unbelief."

The universality of these and related attitudes in all historic forms and experiences of worship belies the notion that tentativeness, as I have described it, is even alien to worship, much less fundamentally opposed to it. The thesis of this chapter is that the principle of polarity between tentativeness and certainty is as essential to significant worship as we have found it to be to theology. In order to clarify and extend this thesis, let us essay two tasks: first, a careful consideration of the nature and aim of worship in general; second, a description of the function of worship in religious living when this is guided by the functional philosophy of value.

THE NATURE AND AIM OF WORSHIP

Evelyn Underhill writes that the only possible formula for worship is this: " I come to adore His splendor, and fling myself and all that I have at His feet." [1] This statement suggests an indispensable characteristic of worship: Worship is an act of adoration, an act in which the part confronts the whole. Through this act the individual gathers himself into an emotional and, in so far as possible, a cognitive unity for the single and express purpose of confronting and adoring the Whole. " I the imperfect adore my Perfect," is Emerson's incisive way of describing the matter. The central aim of worship is adoration. It can and does have many important ethical as well as psychological and physiological consequences, but these are by-products rather than end-considerations. One does not worship in order that he may be a better man. He worships because he has caught a fleeting glimpse of the truth, beauty, goodness, and love resident in life (in his own or someone else's experience) and is impelled by a power more than human to offer up thanksgiv-

[1] *Worship* (New York: Harper & Bros., 1937), p. 9.

ing for them. That this attitude and experience of adoration inevitably result in greater sensitivity and receptivity to God, the value structure of the universe, and thereby determine ethical choices to a greater degree, is at once apparent. Man needs God — that at least is obvious. But he does not worship primarily because of recognition of this need, but rather because he desires to commit himself " body, mind, and soul " to Him whose meanings he has encountered in experience.

Lest we reach or seem to reach the conclusion that worship is merely man's approach to God, it would be well to recall the fact that since Augustine the Christian tradition has steadily insisted that worship is much more than man's strugglings. Miss Underhill is true both to Augustine's insight and to her own convictions when she writes this vigorous warning: " It [worship] is, in fact, a revelation, proportional to the capacity of a creature, of something wholly other than our finite selves, and not deducible from our finite experience: the splendor and distinctness of God. Therefore the easy talk of the pious naturalist about man's approach to God is both irrational — indeed plainly impudent — and irreverent; unless the priority of God's approach to man be kept in mind." [2]

Worship, then, in the traditional Christian sense, is both centered upon God and inspired by him. It is, in short, the response of man to the meanings of God in human experience, to borrow again Dr. W. E. Hocking's famous phrase. Consider Whitehead's description of religion: " Religion is the vision of something which stands beyond, behind and

---

[2] *Ibid.*, p. 6. Cf. W. H. Cadman's statement in *Christian Worship*, N. Micklem, ed. (London: Clarendon Press, 1936), p. 67: " Christian worship is at once the word of God and the obedient response thereto."

within the passing flux of immediate things; something which is real and yet waiting to be realized; something which is a remote possibility and yet the greatest of present facts; something that gives meaning to all that passes and yet that eludes apprehension; something whose possession is the final good and yet is beyond all reach; something which is the ultimate ideal and the hopeless quest." [3]

If this is an accurate description of religion, or better still, to the degree that it is such, the psychologically as well as chronologically primary religious response is one of worship rather than reflection or ethical conduct. [4] Worship is man's reaction to experienced goods, favorable circumstances and enriching experiences: which reaction is not a reveling in the concrete individuality of the experienced goods, favors and values, but is rather an adoring appreciation of their superhuman sources. [5] That the modes of expression utilized are conditioned by the cultural status of the worshiping group is made plain by a study of the history of religions. But beneath and giving validity to the variety of ceremonials is the fundamental and single motif of worship. That worship may be cheap and tawdry is at once apparent. The validity of the standard used in valuation determines the objective worth of the worship reaction. The truer the philosophy of value (whether articulated or not) embedded in the theology implicit in worship, the greater and more enduring is the worth of that worship. [6] But however much worship is dependent for worthfulness upon an adequate philosophy

---

[3] *Science and the Modern World*, p. 275.

[4] Cf. F. von Hügel, *Selected Letters* (New York: E. P. Dutton & Co., 1927), p. 261.

[5] Cf. W. R. Inge, *Christian Ethics and Modern Problems* (New York: G. P. Putnam's Sons, 1930), p. 27: "Homage to the ultimate values is the worship of God."

[6] Cf. Underhill, *op. cit.*, pp. 60, 340–41.

of value, one of its essential characteristics continues to be that of an act of adoration.

Worship, so conceived, demands what Dean Sperry calls "authentic sincerity"[7] — which is infinitely broader than good intentions, meaning, in fact, "a self that has been integrated."[8] Miss Underhill implies this in her vivid phrase, "fling myself and all that I have." We may say that, almost by definition, there is no place in worship for deception, cant and hypocrisy. Worship is not forced upon man whether or no. Man need not adore God. He is not compelled to lift himself as a unit in an act of gratitude. A fair example of what our fathers meant by a "lost soul" is one who experiences the goods of life and regards them either as purely his own creations or as a miserable portion of his just due. This interpretation does not necessarily mean a preachment of quietism, which some claim is an indirect, if not a direct, result of worship. It is pertinent to insist that those who regard worship in this light recognize the sharp distinction that exists between preachments of quietism on the one hand, and admonitions and practices stressing humility on the other. The ethical seers of all ages have combated forms of worship which enshrined such preachments by advancing other forms of worship stressing both the glory of God (or the moral law or the correct order) and the humility of man. This is the logic of religious discovery. Worship is born of appreciation of the values either actually encountered or seen to be implicit, therefore possible, in life. As such it may point with equally clear cogency toward sanctioning, modifying or overthrowing accepted modes of behavior. That the practices of worship, excepting always those periods

---

[7] *Reality in Worship* (New York: The Macmillan Co., 1925), p. 221.
[8] *Ibid.*, p. 205.

when they have been motivated by renewed ethical insight, have invariably sanctioned the existing order of things is better explained by the inertia of traditional patterns of conduct, especially those utilized in releasing high emotional tensions born of crises, than by the nature of worship itself. Worship is as dynamic or static, progressive or regressive, as the philosophy of value which lies at the heart of it.

While Dr. Von Ogden Vogt would doubtless agree that worship is an act of adoration, he suggests another and, at first glance, a more earthy definition of it: " To praise and celebrate life, not merely this good fortune or delivery from that distress, but the memory of all things, the hope of all things, life entire and complete, to praise God and to celebrate his goodness, this is worship." [9]

Although this characterization more patently fits advanced cultures, it calls attention to the synthetic function of worship which is apparent in even the most primitive forms of religious ceremonials. For the worship of primitive man celebrates the vertical as well as the horizontal nature of life. Unquestionably it begins with the horizontal, with the endeavor to unite the individual with his group by calling attention to the communal nature of life processes — birth, growth, food supply and social relationships. But rather than resting content with a comprehensive view of the life enterprise, the worship ceremonial calls attention to certain vertical or perpendicular aspects of life. It delivers the celebrants from the atomism of the present by its use of tradition, scripture and other symbols. The spirits and gods of the group, as well as its heroes, seers and saviors (thought to possess superhuman powers after death) mediated by " old tidings," legends and scripture, become vivid realities

[9] *Modern Worship* (New Haven: Yale University Press, 1927), p. 7.

in the service of worship. The richly symbolic content of vesture, recitations and actions derives from and is hallowed by its rootage in tradition. Although the concepts " spirit " and " gods " are relatively late arrivals in religious thought, the reality indicated by them has been ever with man. For there were aspects of his environment over which he had no actual control: rainfall, climate, disease, storms, etc. It is a short step from the recognition of superhuman powers to the conception of supernatural beings.[10] When and by whom this momentous step was taken in the multiform religious traditions of the world, we have no way of knowing, but that it was taken and that because of it reality was divided into two categories — natural and supernatural — is fairly well agreed upon by historians of religion.[11] For our present purpose its importance lies in its explicit and implicit insistence that the life process is surcharged with meanings that are both objective to man and yet relative to him. The function of worship, then, is not only to integrate or synthesize the individual with his group, and the existent group with its ancestors, but is likewise to dramatize the vital interrelations of the human and the divine, the communal and the cosmic.

Wherever we encounter the act of worship, whether in the primitive dancing around his totem symbol, or in the sophisticate bowing before the miracle of the mass, or in the pantheist singing paeans of praise to nature, it invariably displays three component parts. If and to the extent that any one is absent or minimized, the mood and value of worship are either impoverished or entirely lacking. (1) A belief

---

[10] A. E. Haydon, *Man's Search for the Good Life* (New York: Harper & Bros., 1937), pp. 138 ff.

[11] *Ibid.*, chaps. 5, 6.

in the existence and relevance of an objective reality which man can choose to adore; (2) a profound consciousness of need, of inadequacy and incompleteness, on the part of man; (3) a system of symbols embedded in a dramatic ritual which surrounds the worshiper with vivid suggestions of the vertical as well as the horizontal character of life, the undiscovered as well as the known meanings of God which may yet be experienced and enjoyed by " the humble servant of the way."

It is well to recall that the essential genius of worship is to be found in the fact that it weaves these component parts into the organic unity of an act: dance, liturgy, ritual and pageant. The aim of worship is synthetic rather than analytic, unitive rather than divisive. It takes the arts, sciences and philosophies which at other times are separately pursued each for its own sake and consecrates them to the task of relating man to God. It accepts and utilizes reflection as well as emotion, reason as well as faith, the known as well as the unknown in its dramatization of the relations between man and that aspect — or those aspects — of nature which speaks the final word on all his efforts at defining and satisfying his needs.

THE FUNCTION OF WORSHIP IN RELIGIOUS LIVING

Some philosophy of value — though in primitive religions it is usually so poorly defined that it scarcely amounts to more than a consciousness of value — is the wellspring of all religious endeavor. The preceding chapter sketches the way in which the functional philosophy of value sets itself to interpret the values encountered in daily living. To recapitulate in a sentence, its aim is (1) to discover the nature or structure of value; (2) to discover, as fully as possible, the causal network which accounts for any given value; and (3) to denote as many as possible of the value's meanings in terms of the concrete problems it must face. If this is anything more than another "ivory tower" for philosophy, if it descends into the confusion of life and becomes a factor in influencing choices, loyalties and policies, then it becomes a religious enterprise.

When religion appropriates this or any other philosophy of value, it moves through three stages. As we have seen, philosophical affirmations are translated into theological doctrines. The value structure of the universe is called God and is related to the concrete human problems of failure and frustration, weakness and power, pride and selfishness, hatred and brotherhood. Next, the doctrines are woven into a pattern of worship which strives to sensitize the worshiper to the claims of God. Finally, the doctrines become the major premise of an ethical syllogism, the conclusion of which is a moral "ought" which the believer accepts as indicative of the will of God. Our immediate attention will be restricted to the second stage. The third one will occupy the concluding chapter.

It is the burden of the preceding chapter that the functional philosophy of value does provide the first essential of worship; namely, belief in the existence and relevance of an objective reality which man can choose to adore. Attention is centered upon the nature of value. Values are regarded as organic to nature since they are relationships between natural objects such as man and food, man and man, man and civilization. These relationships are as objectively real as relationships of distance, weight, height, etc., though infinitely more complicated. Another salient characteristic of values is their dynamic formative quality. They are not static entities to be drawn into life as an anchor is drawn into a boat. Rather they are the bright fingers which lay hold of each today and try to guide it in the direction of a more abundant tomorrow. Values are not fragile figurines which shatter into a million pieces when handled roughly. Sometimes they survive, even seem to thrive on, the cruelest batterings of circumstance. At least they do not readily relinquish their hold on life. Aesthetic appreciation does not permit itself to be neglected without violent protest. A friendship never wanes without poignant regrets. When love dies it is almost invariably replaced by cynicism and bitterness. The very fact that war propaganda, to be effective, must show that things have come to such a pass that war and hatred are the only way to demonstrate our loyalty to the ideals of peace and brotherhood is eloquent testimonial to the tenacious nature of these ideals.

From still another angle values are seen to be fraught with cosmic meaning. The process of progressive integration discernible in subhuman levels manifests itself most clearly on the human level in the growth of values. The values truth, beauty, goodness and love are indefinable only when separated from the life processes which give them birth. They denote certain relationships between man and his environment which, if cultivated and furthered, lead toward the abundant life; which, in turn, may be defined as the maximum experience of God open to human beings. To the degree that these values control life it has the strength of genuine purpose, because they are struggling for a fuller realization of themselves in and through the totality of that life.

Man, then, is encompassed by a sea of values some of

which either actually are or may be operative in his experience — such as health, friendship, various loyalties, etc. — others of which may remain forever potential. His environment is far from neutral. He is dependent upon this environing value structure not alone for the creation and preservation of the goods of life that he has, but in addition for the greater goods that may grow in the future.

Religion embraces these philosophical affirmations as evidence supporting belief in the glory and sufficiency of God. This and various other theological doctrines spring from them and are woven into the texture of a worship objective enough to deliver man from the "egocentric predicament" yet vitally relative to the goods and needs of life.

But this message of religion cannot penetrate ears deafened by the amazing yet widespread conceit that man is either entirely or almost self-sufficient, that given a little time and some additional wisdom which will accrue with experience he can get along quite nicely by himself, thank you! Religion has been too constant a companion of man since his emergence on this planet to be deceived by this splendid example of wishful thinking. Consequently the initial aim of the technique of worship is to deflate the human ego and thereby induce a profound consciousness of need which is fundamental to religious discovery and growth. The procedure is simple in nature and universal in scope, though of course variations in detail will conform to differences in cultural and religious traditions. It is equally appropriate in crowded cathedrals and "where two or three are met together" in His name. It confronts the worshiper, through the medium of dramatic ritual, with the sins, extremities and paradoxes of life.

Effective services of worship begin with penitential ut-

terances like " O Lord, be merciful to me a sinner." Aided
by measured chants, hymns and prayers the congregation
not only is reminded of the various sins of man (pride,
selfishness, negligence, hatred), but in addition is given ample opportunity to document, own and confess them. Other
humbling considerations introduced by worship are the unavoidable extremities which all flesh is heir to: sickness, ac-
cident, failure, loss of loved ones, insecurities of one kind or
another, death. Perhaps the most stupendous undertaking
of the ritual of worship in this connection is the presentation of the paradoxes which put human life in its cosmic
setting: time and eternity — the temporal span, the handful
of days of human life in contrast to the eternality of God;
finitude and infinity — man, feeble and circumscribed, set
over against the God of the universe; [12] evil and good —
the petty irritations, the sullen prejudices, the fiery passions
which either arrest or distort growth, seen against the background of those attitudes and activities through which the
constant goodness of God asserts itself.

The Christian religion, as we have seen, centers attention upon the value structure of the world, calling it God,
and insists that the abundant life flows from one type of interaction with this rather than from another. To the strenu-
ous doubter who successfully resists all its efforts to convert
him to this point of view it can only and must finally say:
Try and see. If you can be healthy without conforming,
consciously or not, to the laws of well-being which are implicit in our personalities; if you can enjoy deep friendships
without conforming, consciously or not, to the laws govern-

---

[12] " The eternal miracle of each day is that the God of the universe can use
even me." Statement by Miss Kathrine Duffield, Y.W.C.A. secretary, at the Silver
Bay Y.W.C.A. conference, June, 1934.

ing personal associations which, though we know them in part, are implicit in our structure; if you can create the Great Society, that social structure which seeks to discover, nurture and bring to rich fulfillment the creative energies of man, without paying strict and humble attention to the laws of personal and social growth which are implicit in human beings — in short, if you can succeed in living a full and abundant life governed by the hypothesis that

> I am the master of my fate
> I am the captain of my soul —

then religion has nothing more to say. Religion cannot be seriously challenged by verbal atheism, by the man who says there is no God, but an ax is laid at its roots by ethical atheism, by the man who acts as though there were no God, who regards all the values of life as his own handiwork. Believing as it does that the values that make for abundant living grow in proportion to the degree to which man discovers and conforms to the will of God, the Christian religion sets out deliberately to strip life of those conceits which would keep it self-contained. Its constant endeavor has been to channel the currents of God through the swamps of human self-sufficiency.

Christian worship begins, then, by stressing the fact of sin, man's need for salvation. Its teachings that this world is a "vale of tears," "a house of sin," that "I am a stranger here within a foreign land; my home is far beyond a golden strand," are dramatic ways, appropriate to a definite cultural pattern, of impressing upon man the inadequacy of his own efforts. That these and related pictorial ventures were powerful influences in the day when they were integral aspects of the cultural pattern cannot be doubted. Today they are

" strayed ghosts of an earlier age " and are therefore, when viewed literally, legitimate objects of curiosity.

But we cannot thus easily relegate to a prominent place in the museum of culture the fundamental truth embedded in the Christian doctrine of sin; which may be phrased this way: Whenever, wherever man strikes out on his own as though he has only himself — whether personally, tribally, racially or nationally — to consider in his ethical choices and actions, he is doomed to destruction because the very nature of the universe is opposing him. Underlying, and giving point to, the mythical statement of the doctrine of original sin is the straightforward fact that man is born into the world as an animal organism driven by the desires of self-preservation.[13] The social organization from the beginning devotes its energies toward gratifying these desires and, in his earlier years, requires of him in return a bare minimum of responsibility. But soon the " age of accountability " is reached and society demands recognition of the sense of social solidarity which it has been presenting to him in the form of legend, ritual and belief. Useful though it has been and will continue to be to some degree, if the individual's original equipment endeavors to dominate his maturity as it did his infancy, if he continues to regard all persons and things as means to his own ends, then he is in for the bitter lessons that have been taught men from time immemorial and that we are learning all over again today. Such a person, from the point of view of religion, is in desperate need of salvation because he manifestly thinks more highly of himself than he ought to think. Therefore the Christian religion does

[13] Cf. Gerald Heard, *The Source of Civilization* (New York: Harper & Bros., 1937), for a brilliant critique of the doctrine that " survival of the fittest " has been the way to self-preservation.

not hold the mere fact of life in too high regard. But it has never said, as some of its critics infer, that life is necessarily bad. Rather it has steadily insisted that life with God is good and that life without God is unavoidably bad.

Schleiermacher located the essence of religion in the " sense of dependence "; Hoffding in the "conservation of values." When these insights are coupled and kept together they provide a significant appraisal of the aim of the Christian religion, which is to cultivate in man a sense of his dependence upon God for the conservation and extension of values. For when Christian worship has drained off the poisonous presumptions of man its task is only half done. The other half is to look to God not alone as the author and preserver of all goods, past, present and future, but also as One who redeems from sin. Worship confronts man with the fact of redemption as well as with the fact of sin. It does not heal and redeem, nor does it claim to, but it does strive to unite men with God who is the author of redemption, the source of healing.[14] When worship has sheared from man his presumptions regarding his own sufficiency and has called upon him to turn to God as the One from whom all blessings flow, then its work is ended. Whether the worshiper actually will call upon God for redemption, whether the healing processes of God will produce the results man desires — important as these matters are they lie beyond the reach of worship unless it cares to deal in magical rather than mystical formulas.

Worship, concerned as it is with affirming the twin facts of the need of man and the sufficiency of God, employs the language of symbolism. Symbolism, in general, is the at-

---

[14] Cf. Micklem's paper, " Christian Worship as Reflected in Ancient Liturgies," in his *Christian Worship,* p. 86, where Christian worship is defined from the beginning as the " conscious personal relationship between man and God."

tempt to bring a vast area of meaning within the focus of a sensory image. Social psychology is making increasingly clear the scope and importance of symbolism in social intercourse. Symbols varying from the gesture of an individual to the flag and slogan of a nation comprise the texture of society. Dr. Harold D. Lasswell insists that the first step in unifying the world is the discovery of " efficacious symbols." [15] Every political encounter is replete with examples of how symbols may be used and abused in the heat of controversy. Feelings of love and hate, trust and distrust, joy and sorrow, victory and defeat have appropriate — i.e., socially understood — actions through which they express themselves.

Believing as it does that Jesus is the link between man and God, historic Christian worship has drawn its central symbols more from his person than from his life and teachings. The cross, whether fashioned in wood, iron and gold, or traced over the heart by the finger of the faithful, signifies the redemption of man through the love of God incarnate in Jesus Christ. The Bible is a testimonial to the self-revelation of God in human history, culminating in Jesus Christ, God incarnate in human flesh. The mass, for the devout, symbolizes the continual presence of God in Christ in the church as well as celebrates his actual presence on the altar.

Such symbols do not debate the pros and cons of the meanings they carry; they simply present them to the worshiper. If he is inclined to controversy by them the experience of worship vanishes for him. Questions regarding both the meanings focused in the symbols as well as the adequacy of the symbols themselves have a legitimate place in religion,

[15] *World Politics and Personal Insecurity* (New York: McGraw-Hill Book Co., 1935), pp. 237 ff.

but that place is not in the act of worship. Whether because
he has never questioned them or because he has established
their validity to his own satisfaction, he who would worship
must accept the symbols utilized as adequate foci of the relationship between man and God. Although criticism is
stilled during the act of worship, it is one of the indispensable
prerequisites of continuing vitality. Vital worship demands
ample opportunity both prior and subsequent to the act of
worship for discussion and clarification of the theological
doctrines which validate the symbols used therein.

The tides of change which have swept through the Western world, altering the entire social pattern and with it religious and philosophical formulations, have left their mark
on the central symbols of Christian worship. Historians of
worship are agreed that such symbols (1) are not created by
fiat but rather are emergents (whether products of natural
forces or insertions of supernatural reality is hotly disputed)
in an historical process, and (2) are patently molded by the
same forces which influence the rise, modification and occasional disintegration of theological doctrines. The two earliest sacraments of the Christian fellowship, baptism and the
eucharist, clearly support this view. They did not, like Mi-
nerva daughter of Zeus, come into existence in the full stature
which they were to achieve four centuries later. Baptism
in some form as a rite of purification was insisted upon by
Jewish and Gentile religions alike as the initial step in receiving new members. "From the earliest days, baptism has
been the door into the church." [16] First according to tradition, later according to Scripture, Jesus was baptized by John;
also he gave his disciples power to baptize those who believe.
The early apostles, entering Christianity by way of either

[16] Micklem, "The Sacraments," in his *Christian Worship*, p. 246.

Jewish piety or the Greco-Roman mysteries, practically can-
onized the traditions about Jesus by baptizing their converts.
In this rite, Christianity was not radically different from
many other faiths of the Mediterranean peoples of the first
two centuries of our era.   During the ensuing centuries,
however, the meaning of baptism underwent a marked development paralleling significant changes in the theology
of the faith.   The doctrine of original sin, especially as enunciated by Augustine, made baptism rationally as well as traditionally mandatory for the Christian.   The gradual development and acceptance of the entire sacramental system of
salvation of the church allocated a precise place and meaning
to the inherited rite.[17]

The eucharist presents an even clearer picture of the
growth of a religious symbol.   Beginning in the first century as a meal at the close of day shared by all believers, it
gathered into itself not only the memorial and sacrificial
emphases of the Jewish Passover, but in addition the propri-
atory and god-appropriation strains of the Hellenic mystery
religions.   These three factors — a common meal, Jewish
and Greek ideologies — converged upon (may even have
created) the tradition of Jesus' last meal with his disciples
and made of it the supreme rite of Christian worship.[18]
Miss Underhill gives this terse description of the evolution
of the sacrament: " What we find there [in the New Testa-
ment] is a simple religious rite, on the one hand clearly social, institutional and historical in character — never the act
of the ardent believer, but always that of the group — yet on
the other hand recognized as the sacred means of personal

[17] Article " Baptism," by Hans Leitzmann and John M. Creed, in *Encyclopedia
Britannica* (14th ed.), Vol. III.

[18] C. H. Dodd, " The Sacrament of the Lord's Supper in the New Testament,"
in *Christian Worship*, N. Micklem, ed., pp. 68 ff.

communion between the individual believer and his unseen Lord. Whatever enrichments later practice and reflection may have brought, obedience, remembrance, communion and enhancement of life stand out as features of this primitive corporate experience. As the church gradually came to realize all its implications, so the eucharistic celebration grew in richness and significance; gathering up the largest possible number of spiritual insights and references — both universal and personal — and harmonizing them about its unchanging heart. Into this mold the worshiping instinct of generations has poured itself; and bit by bit there have thus been added to the Christian ritual pattern all those fundamental responses to God which are latent in the religious soul. At last, in the fully developed liturgy, the whole drama of creation and redemption — God's loving movement toward man, and man's response in Christ — is recapitulated; and all the implications which lay hidden in its small origins, the grain of wheat which was flung into the field of the world, are brought to maturity." [19]

Viewed as a whole a liturgy is itself a master symbol which surrounds the worshiper with the profound meanings of the faith and suggests concretely their relevance to human life. The great liturgies of the Christian churches have gone through a definite evolution, the various stages of which are suggested by the writings of students of the subject. [20]

Professor Bartlet writes that " the first or primitive stage of Christian worship, as of Christian thought, was one of free experiment, during which certain modes of expressing the new filial spirit of common devotion inspiring all hearts,

[19] *Op. cit.,* p. 122.

[20] *Ibid.;* Micklem (ed.), *Christian Worship;* Vogt, *op. cit.;* L. Duchesne, *Origins of Christian Worship* (London: Society for the Promotion of Christian Knowledge, 1912).

which had been tested by experience, took shape and attained general acceptance, under the leadership of the most Spirit-gifted." [21] The letters of Paul and Clement, the *Didache* and various other patristic writings are eloquent confirmation of this significant conclusion. Since the first Christian groups were predominantly Jewish and were animated by the conviction that Jesus was the Messiah promised of old, their faith naturally expressed itself in the familiar liturgy of the synagogue worship. So true is this that Dr. Duchesne opines that the eucharist is "the only durable and permanent element which Christianity has added to the liturgy of the synagogues." [22] The simple historical fact that the new faith was soon not only cut adrift from the synagogues but was actively opposed by them and was thereafter under the necessity of interpreting its affirmations to Gentiles should be sufficient reason for the period of "free experimentation."

By the end of the fourth century three factors had emerged which conspired together to determine the content and the general structure of the liturgy for the next fifteen centuries (excepting always the various protestant movements which aimed radically to reform both content and structure of the liturgy). (1) The organization of the church was practically complete. The duties and prerogatives of the clergy were clearly defined; the authority of the bishop of Rome was no longer seriously challenged by other bishops. (2) The New Testament canon was closed and Jerome's biblical labors were putting the Christian Scriptures into approximately their final form. (3) The crucial doctrine of the trinity had been formulated and accepted to the extent

---

[21] Micklem, "Christian Worship as Reflected in Ancient Liturgies," in his *Christian Worship*, p. 85.

[22] Duchesne, *op. cit.*, p. 49.

that it was fundamental to all other theological endeavors, enabling the church for the first time clearly to divide orthodoxy from heresy.

Christian liturgy not so much reflected as actually capitalized these developments. For now its message and congregation of believers were well defined. Its problem henceforth was to relate the unchanging message to changing congregations by means of a pattern of symbols acceptable to both. Its efforts to solve this never-to-be-completely-solved problem have led it through the ages to enlist the aid of every art known to man.

But changes have occurred in both the form and the content of the liturgy. Although Eastern and Western Catholicism share the same fundamental faith in the redemption of man through the intercession of God in Christ, their liturgies stress different aspects of it. Miss Underhill's summary of these differences rewards attention: " The Eastern eucharist is a supernatural mystery, of which the most sacred actions are screened from view. Its devotional emphasis falls upon the coming into time of the Eternal Logos, the unworthiness yet adoring thankfulness of the creature, the awfulness of that which is done. The people are shut off from the sanctuary. . . . All this is in strong contrast with the genius of the true Roman rite, as we find it in the earliest sacramentaries. . . . Here the whole conception is more concrete, more dynamic, even though no less mysterious than in the East. The stress falls not upon the adoring contemplation of the heavenly sacrifice, but upon the due performance here and now of the sacred act, the eucharistic sacrifice in which all take part." [23]

The same author points out that while there has been

[23] *Op. cit.*, pp. 253–54.

some slight adaptation of message to congregation in Eastern Catholicism, there has been an actual evolution within the liturgy of the Western church, an evolution controlled by two factors: " First, the Catholic conception of the church as a living organism, indwelt and guided by the Spirit, and therefore able to grow and change like all other living things; to expand and adjust her worship, and meet the needs of her children, giving fresh expression to the unchanging realities committed to her charge. Second, the concrete and practical character of the Latin mind, which prefers the active to the static and the declared to the mysterious, and is intensely conscious of the temporal order and its limitations and demands." [24]

The protest movements of the Reformation, proceeding as they did by way of sharp break with many vital doctrines of the Catholic Church, strove to construct liturgies that would mediate the reformulated message to congregations of believers set apart from the world by new canons of orthodoxy. In the four hundred years that have elapsed (the same period required for the Catholic liturgy to reach a determinate form) Protestant liturgies have traveled all sorts of roads, varying from Anglican worship with its slight modification of the traditional Catholic worship to the Quaker meetings which utilize a radically different type of symbolism.[25] The search for effective liturgical patterns continues and should continue as long as either the message is modified by science and philosophy or the social controls of the group change.

This basic principle of the efficacious symbol (whether an individual rite or a pattern of symbols) may be discerned in the history of religious symbolism: it must confront the con-

---

[24] *Ibid.,* p. 256.   [25] *Ibid.,* pp. 307 ff.

crete needs of man with affirmations not alone hallowed by tradition but descriptive of certain common experiences as well. And Whitehead with his usual incisiveness leaves the matter this way: "Those societies [*read* churches] which cannot combine reverence to their symbols with freedom of revision must ultimately decay either from anarchy or from the slow atrophy of a life stifled by useless shadows." [26]

The preceding survey, brief though it is, makes it abundantly plain that the Christian churches have not hesitated to alter traditional symbolism in order to communicate old meanings to persons who live in different cultural climates. Some recent historical studies in the meanings of Jesus Christ to successive generations of Christians indicate the adequacy of this conclusion.[27] For, as has been repeatedly said, the symbol Jesus Christ is the central fact in Christian symbolism just as he is the central fact in the theology which undergirds that symbolism. Whether we use the language of art in worship, if it is Christian worship, or the language of philosophy in theology, if it is Christian theology, Jesus Christ is the ultimate focus of meaning. This unalterable and indisputable fact exists wherever the Christian religion, regardless of creed, is found. This, I take it, is one interpretation of the truth of Hebrews' confident affirmation of "Jesus Christ, the same yesterday, today and forevermore." But the studies cited are conclusive on the point that interpretations of what he means have kept pace with variations in the socio-political patterns of the culture of his followers, beginning as early as the differences of opinion between Peter

---

[26] *Symbolism, Its Meaning and Effect* (New York: The Macmillan Co., 1927), p. 88; all of chap. 3 is relevant. Cf. also C. C. Morrison, *The Social Gospel and the Christian Cultus* (New York: Harper & Bros., 1933), *passim*.

[27] Mathews, *The Atonement and the Social Process*; Case, *Jesus Through the Centuries.*

and Paul at Antioch. The history of Christian doctrine, worship and ethics is one of continuous exfoliation, in terms of successive cultures, of the meanings of Jesus Christ.

TENTATIVENESS AND CERTAINTY IN WORSHIP

Two fundamental emphases in the preceding discussion should serve both to illustrate the existence and to demonstrate the importance of the polar relationship between tentativeness and certainty. The first of these is the content of worship which is the dramatization of the vertical, the superhuman, nature of the values of life. Worship begins with concrete experiences of value, yet does not content itself with a narcissistic contemplation of them as things in themselves. Rather it sees in them a revelation of the nature of value itself. It sees in discrete goods the good, in separated occasions of beauty the beautiful, in common acts of fidelity the truth. Worship sees in the values of life God, the Supreme Value, as their creator and sustainer. But worship does not demand complete knowledge of God in order to celebrate him as the source of the values of life. What it does demand is that men shall become sensitive to the presence or absence of values from their experience and what this means to their lives. For values, as we have seen, are dynamic factors in the development of life. They cannot be confined to any given moment but stream into the future as conditioning agents in the choices, loyalties and devotions of men. Worship aims to provide a perspective on values which will enable the worshiper to behold in his daily appreciations, satisfactions and enjoyments experiences which continue as important guides as he enters into the future. Therefore worship endeavors to teach men that the greatest significance of their formulations of truth, beauty, goodness and love, of their idea of

God (all necessarily being based upon past experiences and systematized by more or less careful rational procedure) is as predications of what lies ahead. But alterations in these formulations not only are inevitable but should be welcomed. For God will be supreme value throughout the future as he has been throughout the past. Perhaps the most profound insight of Christian eschatology (belief in the miraculous and cataclysmic intervention of God in history in order to establish his kingdom) is that the God of the past is the God of the future as well. The great liturgies of the church endeavor both to confront their devotees with the mysterious nature of the universe and to inspire confidence in it because, threading it like a firm road through a treacherous swamp, is the purpose of God. Man's struggles to find and follow it have been heartbreaking but not fruitless.

It is clear then that worship as a dramatization of the vertical nature of human values begins with two rock-bottom certainties: (1) the experience of values in the lives of the worshipers; (2) the continuity of these experiences into the future for their fulfillment. But tentativeness supplements each of these certainties. For the value experiences demand articulation and systematization in order to facilitate judgment when one is confronted by new experiences; nor can the accuracy of these formulations, when used as predications of the future, be determined prior to the consequences of their application. It lies with the future whether, or to what extent, they will work. The message of the Christian religion has grown to its present proportions through some such process. It presents each generation with a triple gift: (1) definite assurance drawn from the past; (2) an assimilative power, a broad range of adaptability, which enables it to adjust to present complexities and novelties; (3) confidence in the future. Although it faces the future with diffidence born of the realization that no one knows or can know what is going to happen, it nevertheless affirms that God will take care of his own even though that may mean, in the grim idiom of Calvin, that " some will be damned to the glory of God."

The second emphasis which clarifies the relationship of tentativeness and certainty is closely related to the first. It is the mobile or plastic nature of the symbols of worship. Miss Underhill points out how the implications of the early eucharist were gradually realized as the experience of the Christian group became more comprehensive. The same truth obtains relative to the central symbol of Christian worship — Jesus Christ. It is a palpable untruth to say, as is often done, that he means what men make him mean. No amount of twisting, whether oratorical or legal, can make him a convincing Klansman, or Nordic, or American, though these and similar efforts have been made. The generations of Christians subsequent to his day have followed him not alone because of what he saw and taught but even more truly because of the direction in which he looked and moved. The writer of the Gospel of John puts this pregnant saying in the mouth of Jesus: " Greater things than these shall ye do."

The truth of the matter seems to be this: when men move in the direction in which Jesus looked, they understandably credit him with their discoveries.[28] In Paul's phrase, they " live in Christ." Jesus has become through the centuries the symbol of all good things to all Christian folk. He is variously referred to as the great teacher, preacher, physician, engineer of human life, etc. But the unalterable aspect of

[28] Cf. H. H. Henson, *Christian Morality* (London: Oxford University Press, 1936), chap. 12.

this particular Christian symbol is the direction of living which it indicates. It indicates those attitudes and activities which promote and constitute the abundant life. Therefore, if someone should attempt to make him out a demagogue rather than the great teacher, a dealer in magic rather than the great preacher of righteousness, a destroyer of life rather than the great physician, he would not only be flying in the face of our fragmentary Gospel records, but he would be overwhelmed by the discoveries made by untold multitudes of Christians — common folk as well as mystics, theologians, artists — who through the centuries have faced their future " in Jesus' name."

The point I am trying to make is that religious symbols, along with every other kind, are sensitive to new or changing experiences. Effective symbols grow, and they are effective foci of undiscovered meanings only so long as they do grow. Once more, then, we see the organic relationship between tentativeness and certainty in this process whereby a symbol bearing an accepted meaning acquires new, yet consistent, meanings as it gathers into itself the new experiences of lives inspired by it. Certainty flows (1) from the historical fact which comprises the symbol Jesus of Nazareth, the Lord's Supper, etc. — that there was such a person or original event; (2) from the growing body of meanings attributed to it by subsequent worshipers — it has meant *this* to our fathers; (3) from the definite nature (what I have been calling direction) of the symbol by virtue of which it accepts some meanings and rejects others — to adore him, or participate in it, one must do certain things. Tentativeness enters all along the line because all three of these sources of certainty not only are born of empirical data but for continued significance constantly rely upon them. And, as we have seen, empirical judgments for their very life depend upon tentativeness. It alone can keep the past experience sensitive to the meanings of present and future.

Worship without the expectancy of greater light about to break forth from God, without the agonized groping for a clearer vision of the deepest meanings of life, is indistinguishable from magic. Where worship is the living edge of religious faith it continues to perform its historic function of leading men in an act of adoration of the goodness of God upon whose mercies they are dependent.

X

SYNTHESIS OF TENTATIVENESS
AND CERTAINTY IN ETHICAL CONDUCT

LIFE IS fundamentally, even brutally, pragmatic. It may be characterized as an unending flow of related tensional situations which make a common demand upon all participants — they must act and react. Ideas and ideals, concepts and plans, philosophies and religions are thrown into a hopper that is alive with action, and their worth is measured not by their brilliance in detachment but by the extent to which their influence is discernible in consequences of action. When a student once characterized Sir Thomas More's *Utopia* as " a good idea but it won't work," he elicited this reply from Dr. James Hayden Tufts: " Young man, I trust you will soon learn life's fundamental lesson: if it is a good idea it will work and if it won't work it isn't a good idea." Granting that the meaning of " work " is exceedingly difficult to fasten down, we must recognize that the ethical insights of the Jewish-Christian religion have always had some such aim; their relevance to life has been one of their strongest appeals. It is not distorting the facts to affirm that with all the otherworldliness involved in the creation and coddling of rationalistic and mystical absolutes, this particular religious tradition is prepared to deal with the pragmatic quality of life.

In order to clarify the terms which will be used, let us recall that morality concerns itself with the standards which regulate the life of a people. It accepts, institutionalizes, defends and perpetuates these standards. Ethics has two functions, both of which root in, yet transcend, morality. Descriptive or comparative ethics deals with the comparison and clarification of the various standards operative in different moralities. Normative ethics builds upon this work and seeks to determine what the ideal standards are, what the goals and ideals of action ought to be. It is in the latter sense that we shall be using the phrase " ethical conduct " in this chapter — as action which aims to translate the " is " of life into the " ought-to-be "; more accurately, perhaps, to discover that way of relating the " is " to the " ought-to-be " by virtue of which the latter increasingly informs the former.

It is within the area of ethical action, so conceived, that the polarity between tentativeness and certainty in religion is subjected to severest strain. If we could meet the requirements of life simply by reflecting on what ought to be done, our present problem would never arise. But we are called upon to live in line with such reflections. We are held responsible for the ideals which motivate our actions. When we try to live in line with them we find that almost without exception our ideals and plans are roughly handled by life-situations; certainly they are never more than crude approximations of the value structure encountered in life. The least we can say is that the realities of life have successfully resisted every attempt of science, religion and philosophy to discern an all-pervasive unity among them. Philosophy's " rationality of the universe," science's " uniformity of nature," and religion's " omnipotence of God " are classic examples of good horses that were ridden too far. There are, or seem to be, exceptions to these generalizations in sufficiently large numbers to modify them rather than to prove them the rule.

But however roughly life may deal with our ideals, ideas and plans, we shall continue to use them, suffer with them, improve them, and use them again; and all this because they constitute our only insurance against aimlessness. They are essential ingredients of purposive activity. Yet they are not ultimates in the sense that we must accept them without inquiry and cling to them regardless of consequences in order to be guided by them. If they were, then tentativeness would indeed be the enemy of religion. Our problem is this: Can the ideal defined as an instrument of discovery command sufficient loyalty to evoke ethical action? How far is it possible, or is it possible, for a person to accept as the controlling factor in his choices and planning a formulation which he knows will be redefined in the light of experience?

Religion in its creative moments (those to which subsequent generations cling as times when God was close to man) has not been deceived into an idolatry of ideals. It has regarded them as improvable equipment. "Ye have heard it said by them of old time, but I say unto you. . . ." Ideals are valuable in so far and only in so far as they are expressions of God's will. The ethical strand in the Jewish-Christian religion, distinguished for the moment from the mystical and rational emphasis, has always placed its final confidence not in ideals as such, but in the consequences of activity guided and sustained by religious ideals. While the rationalists strove for logical coherence in religious formulations and the mystics sought the "peace that passeth all understanding," the ethical seers have confronted both with the insistence that the final validation of logically coherent religious formulations and the experience of mystic ecstasy inheres in ethical action. "Not everyone that saith . . . but he that doeth. . . ."

Prophetic religion, as outlined by J. M. P. Smith in *The Prophet and His Problems*,[1] is one such creative moment in our religious tradition; for in the eighth and seventh centuries before Christ sensitive religious spirits were struggling toward newer and more adequate conceptions of religion in a way strangely akin to that of our own day. When the radical Christian leaders of today [2] revitalize and redefine Christian ideals by interpreting them in terms of social problems they are following in the path marked out by the seers of early Israel who strove to make their religious inheritance live again by stating it in ethical "ought's." "Their [prophets'] service was . . . in finding a new application for old truths and preeminently in the exaltation of ethics to its rightful place in the scheme of things.[3] . . . It is the glory of the prophet at his best that he allowed nothing to share the place that belonged of right to ethics alone. He enthroned ethics in the very heart of Yahweh and thus made Yahweh the God of the universe. . . . This was not a philosophical or a speculative but an ethical monotheism."[4] Thus we find these men of God who were "called of God, inspired of God, and sustained of God"[5] actually speaking for God, counseling their hearers to "let judgment run down as waters and righteousness as a mighty stream";[6] "sow to yourselves in righteousness";[7] "to do justly, to love mercy, and to walk humbly with thy God";[8] "wash you, make you clean; put away the evil of your doing from before mine eyes; cease to do evil, learn to do well."[9]

---

[1] New York: Charles Scribner's Sons, 1923, pp. 209 ff.

[2] Reinhold Niebuhr, John Bennett, Gregory Vlastos, Bishop F. J. McConnell, Arthur E. Holt, Shailer Mathews, C. C. Morrison.

[3] J. M. P. Smith, *op. cit.*, p. 220.

[4] *Ibid.*, p. 222.

[5] *Ibid.*, p. 211.

[6] Amos 5:24.

[7] Hos. 10:12.

[8] Mic. 6:8.

[9] Isa. 1:16–17.

The prophets had no quarrel with the rubric of temple worship, feast and fast days, Sabbaths and sacrifices, except as concern for these edged ethical action out of the focus of attention. They most assuredly did not scrap the ideals embedded in traditional religion, though they did redefine and expand them. Purity before God was one such ideal. Too frequently it had meant bringing the correct sacrificial offering, etc. Micah, too, believed in purity before God, but he drove it to the heart of the universe with the staggering — and unanswerable — question, "Shall I count them pure with the wicked balances and with the bag of deceitful weights?"[10]

The holiness of God is the accepted fundamental of prophetic religion wherever it appeared in ancient Israel, a conception shared with the great figures of the priestly tradition — Moses, Ezekiel, Ezra. The uniqueness of the prophets lies in their perception and enunciation of the fact that divine holiness inserts itself into human affairs as ethical commandments to seek and promote righteousness. "Who shall ascend into the hill of the Lord? or who shall stand in his holy place? He that hath clean hands, and a pure heart; who hath not lifted up his soul unto vanity, nor sworn deceitfully. He shall receive the blessing from the Lord, and righteousness from the God of his salvation."[11]

Students of the Gospels agree that Jesus felt the full force of the prophetic tradition and, accepting its ethical emphasis, he gave it its supreme expression. Reinhold Niebuhr asserts, "The ethic of Jesus is the perfect fruit of prophetic religion."[12] Dr. B. W. Robinson says that the "best attested

[10] Mic. 6:11.
[11] Ps. 24:3–5.
[12] *An Interpretation of Christian Ethics* (New York: Harper & Bros., 1935), p. 37.

saying " of Jesus (in that it occurs six times in the Gospels) is this: " Anyone who aims to preserve his own self will lose his soul, but anyone who loses himself in the cause of the gospel will find himself." [13]   Significantly, in one case this counsel concludes Jesus' instructions to the twelve as he sends them out as missionaries.   Albert Schweitzer feels that in this tenth chapter of Matthew we have the actual words of Jesus.[14]   Be that as it may, one characteristic of Jesus was his constant calling of men into a life of purposive activity, designed to demonstrate their fitness for the Kingdom of God. There is an urgency, almost a ruthlessness, in his imperious insistence that men should leave homes, families, work, should cut across fundamental strictures of the reigning morality in order to do the will of God.

Scholars have argued, without conclusiveness, that this is an " interim ethic " — one especially devised to guide life during the last days of the world.   Whether, or to what extent, this is true is an important question, and it is emerging as a contemporary problem in the current edition of the eschatological ethic espoused by Paul Tillich [15] and Reinhold Niebuhr [16] and fondled by John Bennett.[17]   Our present purpose does not require us to take sides, since the contestants are in agreement on the essential nature of that ethic though they differ on the intended scope of its applicability.   For Jesus, obedience to the will of God is of supreme importance, and this obedience is fundamentally and unalterably ethical.

[13] *The Sayings of Jesus* (New York: Harper & Bros., 1930), p. 145.   Cf. Mark 8:35; Luke 9:24 and 17:33; Matt. 10:39 and 16:25; John 12:25.

[14] *The Quest of the Historical Jesus* (New York: The Macmillan Co., 1925), p. 357.

[15] *The Religious Situation of the Present* (New York: Henry Holt & Co., 1932), p. 143; *The Interpretation of History*, pp. 266 ff.

[16] Numerous writings, especially *An Interpretation of Christian Ethics,* chap. 2.

[17] *Social Salvation* (New York: Charles Scribner's Sons, 1935), chap. 5.

As Professor E. R. Scott puts it, " He came with a message from God, and his ethic has no meaning apart from his religion." [18] Leslie Stephen argues that Jesus' great discovery, the one provoking the moral revolution of Christianity, is that "morality is internal," [19] that he was urging men to "'be this' instead of 'do this.'" Granting at once that Jesus played havoc with existing catalogues of virtuous and evil acts by calling attention to motive, that his emphasis upon the vicious nature of lust and hate was understandably startling to men who preened themselves upon not having committed adultery and murder, the fact remains that Jesus nowhere separates motive from consequences, character from conduct. He was striving to re-establish the inner pole of ethical action when he taught his disciples that the great evils of life come from within: " That which cometh out of the man, that defileth the man. For from within, out of the heart of man, proceed evil thoughts, adulteries, fornications, murders, thefts, covetousness, wickedness, deceit, lasciviousness, an evil eye, blasphemy, pride, foolishness: all these evil things come from within, and defile the man." [20] We do violence to Jesus' ethic unless we have a clear perception of the fact that he was teaching men that you cannot gather " grapes from thorns, or figs from thistles "; that " a good tree cannot bring forth evil fruit, neither can a corrupt tree bring forth good fruit." [21] But equal violence is done when we separate this emphasis from the famous judgment scene when men are divided into sheep and goats according to their deeds.[22] Jesus proclaims the prophetic ideal of purity

[18] *Ethical Teachings of Jesus* (New York: The Macmillan Co., 1924), p. xii.
[19] *The Science of Ethics* (London: Smith, Elder & Co., 1882), p. 155.
[20] Mark 7:20–23.
[21] Matt. 7:18.
[22] Matt. 25:31–46.

before God ("blessed are the pure in heart, for they shall see God") and insists that ethical action is an inevitable consequence of it, is, indeed, the token by which it is recognized. He shares the prophetic faith that the holiness of God lays man under severe ethical requirements. "Therefore, if thou bring thy gift before the altar, and there rememberest that thy brother hath aught against thee; leave there thy gift before the altar, and go thy way; first be reconciled to thy brother, and then come and offer thy gift." [23]

How much Paul knew of the life and teachings of Jesus we do not know. His associations with Luke and Mark as well as his frequent contacts with the disciples establish the strong probability that he knew considerably more than comes to expression in any of his writings that survive. Why he does not make more use of his knowledge is a matter of conjecture. He could not have thought lightly of it. Deissmann summarizes the problem this way: "The earthly life of Jesus, then, was appreciated by Paul, at least in the letters that have come down to us, more for its character as a whole than for its details. . . . That Paul is influenced generally by the tradition of the words of Jesus, even when he does not expressly quote them, is shown by the moral exhortations of his letters and by other silent adaptations of sayings of Jesus. . . . In his oral preaching mission the apostle no doubt made a still more ample use of the words of Jesus than was necessary in letters directed to Christians. . . . At the commanding center, however, of Paul's contemplation of Christ stands the Living One who is also the Crucified, or the Crucified who is also alive." [24]   This, then, is the pattern through

---

[23] Matt. 5:23–24.
[24] *Paul* (New York: Doubleday, Doran & Co., 1926), pp. 195 ff.

which the prophetic emphasis upon ethical action comes to expression in Paul.[25]

The apostle in his many-sided writings expresses the firm belief that salvation comes to those who accept Jesus as the revelation of God, who live in Christ and in whom Christ lives. Such salvation yields a "new creature in Christ," which is as truly an ethical as a mystical transformation. For Paul constantly insists that there are definite "fruits of the spirit" that give indubitable evidence of the indwelling of Christ in the heart of the believer. Such fruits are profoundly ethical: "love, joy, peace, long-suffering, gentleness, goodness, faith, meekness, temperance . . . and they that are Christ's have crucified the flesh with the affections and lusts." [26] To be born again, with new desires, appetites and passions, to want to love Christ and serve him only — this is the fruit of salvation for Paul.

AUTHORITARIAN RELIGIOUS ETHICS

Historically, Christian ethics has been authoritarian in structure rather than empirical, though empiricism has never been wholly absent. The difference in emphasis between the two is marked and may be stated this way: Authoritarian religious ethics provides, or claims to provide, revelation of infallible choice, whereas empirical religious ethics guarantees nothing beyond intelligent choosing. The three most important sources of infallible authority holding sway in Christendom are church, Bible, and conscience or the inner light. Wherever these have been accepted authoritarianism in ethics was and is inevitable. Whether it is a Catholic and his church or a Protestant and his Bible or a Quaker and his inner guid-

[25] Inge, *op. cit.*, p. 39.   [26] Gal. 5:22–24.

ance, they share a single conviction, namely, that they possess certain knowledge of what to do, how to act and what to choose.

The Catholic Church has indicated in characters so bold that " he who runs may read " that the way to salvation involves correct theological beliefs and ecclesiastical conformity. This type of authoritarianism utilizes a straight-away deductive approach to ethical action. For the major premise of its ethical syllogism is always compounded of its doctrines of man, God, sin and salvation. These are above question, since they are revealed truth. The minor premise asserts that the concrete problem faced by the perplexed person is an instance of the subject of the major premise. The conclusion inevitably follows, deriving from the predicate of the major premise. This is a fair illustration of the procedure:

> All invasion of divine prerogatives is sin.
> Birth control by means of artificial contraceptives is an invasion of divine prerogatives.
> Therefore, this type of birth control is sin.

Waiving the mare's nest of difficulties inherent in the initial statement, the crux of the problem manifestly is in the minor premise; for it is possible to argue with considerable cogency that there are many situations in which birth control by any and every means constitutes, so far as human wisdom can see, a support of God's will, assuming that he is interested in creating and supporting the abundant life.[27] The reason for using this particular illustration is not to provoke argument on birth control, but rather to indicate that authoritarian religious ethics always operates in an area of uncertainty

---

[27] Inge, *op. cit.*, pp. 283–84, gives some shocking illustrations in support of this point.

when it strives to relate its infallible principles to empirical problems.[28]

It would seem that, bolstered by the imposing ecclesiastical organization, surrounded by the all-inclusive intricacies of theology, and brooded over by the watchful eye of one who had immediate and efficacious access to the will of God and the church alike, ethical action should have been an open and closed affair for the Catholic. Such, however, has not been the case. The category of purgatory may be regarded as an eternal and fitting commemoration of the hiatus between the revealed wisdom, the bestowed power of the authoritative church, and the particular problems of the individual. Much as Plato's philosopher stumbles when he returns from gazing on absolute good to the half-lights of existence in which his fellows dwell, the church has blundered along from case to case, culture to culture, age to age. As John Dewey points out, " one of the most instructive things in all human history is the system of concessions, tolerances, mitigations and reprieves which the Catholic Church with its official supernatural morality has devised for the multitude." [29] Dr. Dewey feels that this is a concession to the inability of the multitude to adhere to a lofty ethic. Without doubt there is some truth in this position, but a more obvious reason is that the ethical principles which were crystal-clear and self-evident while undisturbed in the enfoldment of theological and ecclesiastical authority, were neither clear nor self-evident when applied to concrete cases. In support of this interpretation, we should remember that the " system of concessions, etc." to which Dr. Dewey refers is administered by the priest to the laymen through the medium of the confessional; which,

---

[28] Cf. Chap. IV.
[29] *Human Nature and Conduct* (Modern Library Series), p. 5.

viewed abstractly, is the moment when the authoritarian
ethics of the church meets empirical problems.

Consider, for further light on the relationship between
authoritarian religious ethics and concrete cases, the most
courageous and incisive attempts of the Roman Catholic
Church to deal with social and economic problems: the encyclicals *Rerum Novarum* of Pope Leo XIII, issued in 1891,
and *Quadragesimo Anno* of Pope Pius XI, issued in 1931.[30]
Both, especially the former, are profoundly rich in ethical
principles drawn from the theology of the church and her
long heritage of experience.

Rerum Novarum, after a telling description of the " misery
and wretchedness which press so heavily at this moment on
the large majority of the poor," [31] and a treatment — all too
inadequate — of the socialists' view of property,[32] proceeds to
discuss " man's natural right to private property," [33] and
" man's natural right and his social and domestic duties." [34]
Having defined these natural rights, the document is prepared to define, *in general,* " the Christian interdependence
of capital and labor." Two sections on this subject, though
lengthy, deserve quotation:

" First of all, there is nothing more powerful than religion
(of which the church is the interpreter and guardian) in
drawing rich and poor together, by reminding each class of
its duties to the other, and especially of the duties of justice.

" Thus religion teaches the laboring man and the workman
to carry out honestly and well all equitable agreements freely

---

[30] Both encyclicals are given, with comments, in that excellent volume by
Father Husslein, *The Christian Social Manifesto* (New York: Bruce Publishing Co.,
1931). The encyclicals are divided into sections and numbered accordingly; we
shall refer to the encyclical by initials and to the section by number.

[31] *R. N.,* 2.   [33] *R. N.,* 5–6.

[32] *R. N.,* 3–4.   [34] *R. N.,* 9–12.

made, never to injure capital, nor to outrage the person of an employer; never to employ violence in representing his own cause, nor to engage in riot and disorder; and to have nothing to do with men of evil principles, who work upon the people with artful promises, and raise foolish hopes which usually end in disaster and in repentance when too late.

"Religion teaches the rich man and the employer that their work people are not their slaves; that they must respect in every man his dignity as a man and as a Christian; that labor is nothing to be ashamed of, if we listen to right reason and to Christian philosophy, but is an honorable employment, enabling a man to sustain his life in an upright and creditable way; and that it is shameful and inhuman to treat men like chattels to make money by, or to look upon them merely as so much muscle or physical power. Thus, again, religion teaches that, as among the workmen's concerns are religion herself, and things spiritual and mental, the employer is bound to see that he has time for the duties of piety; that he be not exposed to corrupting influences and dangerous occasions; and that he be not led away to neglect his home and family or to squander his wages. Then, again, the employer must never tax his work people beyond their strength, nor employ them in work unsuited to their sex or age.

"His great and principal obligation is to give to every one that which is just. Doubtless before we can decide whether wages are adequate, many things have to be considered, but rich men and masters should remember this — that to exercise pressure for the sake of gain, upon the indigent and destitute, and to make one's profit out of the need of another, is condemned by all laws, human and divine. To defraud anyone of wages that are his due is a crime which cries to the avenging anger of heaven. 'Behold, the hire of the laborers . . . which by fraud has been kept back by you, crieth; and the cry of them hath entered the ears of the Lord of Sabaoth.' Finally, the rich must religiously refrain from cutting down the workman's earnings, either by force, fraud, or by usurious dealings; and with the more reason because the poor man is weak and unprotected, and because his slender means should be sacred in proportion to their scantiness. Were these precepts carefully obeyed and followed, would not strife die out and cease? " [35]

I doubt whether authoritarianism in ethics can ever come to closer grips with concrete realities than Pope Leo XIII does in these passages. Yet the careful reader will find their crucial concepts, those designed to unite the regulative principles deduced from theology with concrete evils, incapable of systematic and precise definition. Consider the following: equitable agreements, violence, disorder, evil principles, slaves, Christians, right reason, corrupting influences, dangerous occasions, to give to everyone that which is just, usurious. A later section in the same encyclical defines a fair wage as " remuneration . . . enough to support the wage earner in reasonable and frugal comfort." [36] That such regulative principles meet concrete realities in an area of uncertainty is recognized by implication, at least, first in the admission that " doubtless before we can decide whether wages are adequate, many things have to be considered," and second in the recommendation that workingmen's associations be multiplied, [37] one of whose functions would be to decide disputes [38] over matters pertaining to fair wage, " hours of labor in different trades, the sanitary precautions to be observed in factories and workshops." [39]

[35] *R. N.,* 16–17.
[36] *R. N.,* 34.
[37] *R. N.,* 36. Cf. Husslein, *op. cit.,* chaps. 29 and 33.
[38] *R. N.,* 43.
[39] *R. N.,* 34.

Both encyclicals agree in leaving technical matters to technicians and experts, though neither term is clarified. Presumably ethical action will result when owners and workingmen, both immersed in relevant concrete facts, attack mutual problems with the aid of experts and under the guidance of the regulative principles so clearly enunciated by the popes. We shall have cause to see that no criticism can fall upon this general procedure, except possibly the most inclusive criticism of all, namely, that fundamentally it is then not an authoritarian religious ethic but is implicitly empirical and experimental.

Though Protestant groups have transferred the base of authority from the church to Scripture and conscience, the logical form of ethical reasoning has been unchanged. Reliance upon scriptural authority covers the wide range from biblical literalism to the liberal valuation of the Bible as an invaluable deposit of religious experience.

Biblical literalism (more commonly called fundamentalism) believes the Bible to be the infallible word of God. It regards the Scriptures as a sort of pipe-line carrying " all we know on earth and all we need to know," and holds that the whole function of religious leadership is to find, by means of minute textual scrutiny, new places for tapping the line and making its contents available for concrete problems. The all-time low in the absurdity to which this procedure is liable was reached, not when Paul was quoted against bobbed hair, Leviticus against knickers for women, etc., but when a state representative in the Illinois legislature argued against prohibition by leading a parade through the august chamber of the house, waving the Book before his listeners and quoting Paul's admonition to Timothy to " take a little wine for the stomach's sake." The horns of the beasts in Daniel have practically disappeared under the constant polishings of those who insist upon reading therein preconceived meanings. The long succession of men, from Nero to Hitler, Mussolini and Stalin, who have confidently been proved to be the Antichrist of Revelation is sufficient commentary upon the logical procedure. For our immediate purpose it is sufficient to note the extraordinary fluidity of the biblically grounded lists of virtues and vices. Such lists vary, not with our increasing knowledge of the socio-religious backgrounds of the Bible, but with changes in our environment.

It does not require more than a casual survey of the Christian world today to reach the conclusion that this way of using the Bible not only has brought discredit upon the Bible but is on its way out. Few if any denominational colleges accredited by recognized accrediting agencies present the Bible in this fashion. Ranting evangelism continues to espouse it; occasional startled laymen like the late William Jennings Bryan leave fruitful work in other fields and fly to its rescue to awaken only pity for their efforts rather than secure conviction for the cause; its magician-like manipulation of biblical materials convinces only those who are prepared to believe. Perhaps the most conclusive consideration is that scholars after the order of the late John Gresham Machen are few and far between in its ranks, and without such men to orient its case to the perplexities of men neither this nor any other point of view can hope effectively to condition social behavior. Of course, biblical literalism has no more than a passing interest in ethical action; it has, in fact, roundly scored the merely moral man as an enemy of God.

It is pertinent to indicate one significant historical fact about the social gospel movement of the past half-century that has been noted so often that any elaboration of it is unnecessary. Biblical literalism not only did not produce the movement, but as a matter of fact had little to do with it. In this movement we see one significant difference between biblical literalism and biblical liberalism. For the social gospel movement flowed from the springs of liberalism, and, with all its delusions about progress, surrender to the emerging secularism, etc., it remains the one concerted effort of Protestantism to rise above denominationalism in the attempt to elicit ethical action in terms of social problems. Its social idealism continues to find pungent expression in the pronouncements of its institutional heir, the Federal Council of the Churches of Christ in America.

Since ethical action rooting in biblical liberalism is more empirical than authoritarian, fuller consideraton of it will be postponed to the next section.

A conscience-guided ethic is the remaining form of authoritarianism which religion has espoused. Conscience, though difficult of definition, is identified by its dependence for direction upon revelations which are profoundly personal mystical contacts with God or some substructure of eternal law. Professor T. V. Smith gives conscience, so conceived, the trenchant appellation " a divine outpost." [40] His significant book may be regarded as demonstrating the fact that conscience is not an ultimate in ethical theory, since its dicta are no sounder than the authoritative base upon which they rest. Theorists in ethics from Socrates to Professor T. V. Smith have advanced many different bases for the deliverances of conscience. There is no call for our entering the lists of this debate; we take leave of it, accepting its unanimous affirma-

[40] *Beyond Conscience* (Chicago: University of Chicago Press, 1934), p. 32.

tion that conscience is a mediator between man and something else.[41]

An example of this mediation is found in the foundation
of Kantian morality, "the moral law within," which underlies and validates the dicta of conscience. Yet the Christian
religion refuses to accept the moral law as an ultimate and
insists that it must be validated as the will of God (in Thomistic language, as an expression in nature of an eternal law)
or go without validation. While most Christian thinkers
have not been as pessimistic about man's moral nature as
Augustine and Calvin, they have, without exception, been
wary of intuition-guided activity such as is implied in the
doctrine of conscience. Mysticism, or what Troeltsch calls
"spiritual religion," as distinct from organized religion in
the church and the social radicalism of the sect, alone has extended it a friendly hand. Troeltsch defines mysticism as
"simply the insistence upon a direct inward and present
religious experience."[42] Its aim is to produce a personal
communion between man and God describable only as un-
speakable ecstasy. It makes constant capital of the fact that
Christianity began as a religion of personal salvation mediated through Christ in whom one might be in unbroken
communion with God.[43]

This profound and powerful emphasis upon religion as
personal communion was stifled, at least severely minimized,
during the great ages of rationalism and ecclesiasticism in
religion; yet it was constantly siring "brotherhood move-

[41] Dr. Smith's own conclusion, however, is no conclusion at all, since for him
conscience is a heroic gesture, the self speaking as an aesthetic unity. This simply
raises the problem of the nature of a self capable of reacting in this way; so we
find ourselves once more confronted with the validation of conscience.

[42] *Social Teachings of the Christian Churches* (New York: The Macmillan
Co., 1931), II, 730.

[43] Deissmann calls this *Christusmystik*.

ments " of one sort and another. It is a striking fact that every great monastic or conventual order began in the person of some one or ones who strove to transcend the rational, social character of church and sect religion and achieve intuitive, personal intimacy with God. Evelyn Underhill's work, *The Mystics of the Church,* contains ample evidence supporting this view.[44] She finds that the mystics seldom break with accepted theological doctrines and ecclesiastical practices; rather they aim to bring the life and warmth of religion into them by means of discovering the way or ways of personal communion with God.

Not all reform movements born of the desire to deepen the spirituality of the church succeeded in staying within it. The tragic story of the Albigenses and Waldenses is in vivid contrast to that of the clerical and lay groups who were accepted by the church. Protestantism has found it as difficult as Catholicism to pour the new wine of a spiritually grounded reform into the old wineskins of acceptable theology and polity. Methodism and Quakerism illustrate the matter. The former from the beginning has aimed at the creation of a strong church, with clear theological doctrine and accepted liturgical practice, though it has usually permitted a margin for difference of opinion. Quakerism, however, has consistently tried to avoid developing either theological or ecclesiastical traditions. It has clung to its principle of guidance through the inner light, and therefore furnishes the most authentic case of an endeavor to construct a conscience-guided ethic. Keeping fully in mind the Friends' distaste for theology and church polity, one must nevertheless observe that it is not accurate to say that the various ethical policies of the group root in the deliverance of conscience alone.

[44] New York: Doubleday, Doran & Co., 1926.

Their stand against war, for example, grows from their doctrine — and doctrine it is in fact if not in name — of the brotherhood of man; which doctrine, in turn, is bolstered by the New Testament teaching on nonviolence and love.[45] Thus we see the inevitable tendency of conscience to validate its deliverances by resting them, at least partially, upon some *social,* i.e. shareable, base.　William Penn puts the point positively when he challenges the Quakers' critics thus: "You profess Holy Scriptures: but what do you witness and experience?　What interest have you in them?　Can you set to your seal that they are true by the work of the same spirit in you that gave them forth in the holy ancients?"[46]　We have in this succinct statement the "something else" which conscience mediates to man, namely, the spirit of God revealed in Scripture, yet discernible there only by one in whose life it is a present experience.　Hence if the inner light be regarded as light rather than darkness, it is because the one in whom it glows gives full credence to the belief in the continuing presence of God.

All known cases of mystical or spiritual religion have given rise to some form of rationalization (explanation and interpretation) and have invested themselves in institutions of more or less rigid natures.　Indeed we write of this form of religion only in terms of such developments.　Troeltsch's analysis of the origins of spiritual religion prepares us for his cryptic summary of its ability to deal with concrete ethical issues:

" Spiritual religion or mysticism is not a product of particular social conditions.　It proceeds from other causes: the ex-

---

[45] "They [the Quakers] . . . took the Sermon on the Mount as their ethical ideal." — Troeltsch, *op. cit.,* p. 781.

[46] *A Summons or Call to Christendom,* quoted in article " Friends, Society of," *Encyclopedia Britannica* (14th ed.), IX, 851.

perience of the incapacity of the churches to realize their ideal, weariness of the strife and conflict of religious parties, the pure inner dialectic of religious feeling returning to its ultimate source, the critical destruction of dogmas and cults, and weariness of the disappointments and confusions of the external life in general. Its inner circles do not penetrate into the masses, and its purely contemplative ideas do not grip the common life, but work purely personally, or hover in a literary manner over the whole. In modern times certainly, its extension depends upon the existence of classes which live apart from the crude struggle for existence, and can seek spiritual refinement for their own sake, so far as it is not hidden in small evangelical sects, which also, however, have always a special sectarian trait. Beyond that it is connected with the modern scientific cultivation of the autonomous reason, in so far as this takes a religious turn. To this extent it reflects today the universal individualism of modern times, which indeed it still further strengthens. It accompanies social conditions, but does not arise out of them, nor does it influence them directly. Indirectly, however, the fact that it weakens the power and exclusiveness of the churches means that it has a very important social influence." [47] And the conclusion of the matter is this: " The usual answer [given when conduct is questioned], ' The Spirit recognizes the Spirit,' was found to be useless in practice. Hence this standpoint easily led to the giving up of all and every kind of organized fellowship, or to a withdrawal into private groups of a purely personal character composed of kindred souls." [48]

As long as spiritual religion remains an inward experience it is unrelated to ethical idealism; it is simply and solely the ecstatic experience of reabsorption into deity. But the exi-

---

[47] Troeltsch, *op. cit.*, pp. 816–17.   [48] *Ibid.*, p. 999.

gencies of life summon the mystic back to the social milieu. It is then that he must make an important decision: he may admit that the experience is ethically irrelevant; he may beat a retreat from as many as possible of the problems pressing for solution; he may grope toward an application of the experience and call upon church, theology, Scripture or some other social aid for help. Historically all three alternatives have been adopted at some time or other; the second has been far and away the most usual development, furnishing the motif for all ascetic movements which have sought to segregate themselves from the world; the third amounts to admission that inner guidance, alone, is unable to cope with ethical realities.

The judgment, therefore, is based upon experience when we say that conscience or the inner light taken by itself is a wholly unreliable basis for ethical action. In and of itself it tends either to insulate the individual from the urgency of moral problems or to fling him into social action under the guidance of a standard which is essentially incommunicable and beyond social validation, and therefore incapable of coming to grips with empirical realities, which, as we have seen, are hemmed in by unavoidable uncertainties and relativities. Ethical action, motivated by uncritical reliance upon conscience, is bound to assume some form of anarchism, resulting in the denial of normal social intercourse through the creation of an esoteric social group based upon fellowship in the Spirit. The very fact that mystics have gravitated into societies and orders is perhaps the final answer to the claim that their intuitive insights are all-sufficient. The slow but sure evolution of the governing doctrines of mystical societies, such as the Quakers and the contemporary Oxford movement, must be regarded as evidence for the fact that conscience, or any other form of " guidance " of the person by God, must, if it is to influence behavior, let alone perpetuate itself, depend upon social implementation in the form of doctrines and an organization which endeavor to interpret its meaning to believers as well as to communicate it to un-believers. Conscience, as a conviction of the validity and authenticity of an insight, is undoubtedly an important factor in convincing ethical action, but it is not self-sufficient. It must be bolstered by regulative principles drawn from some other source, whether theology, tradition, Scripture, or past experience as it is gathered together in traditional morality. Conscience is not an ultimate in ethical action, though it is an indispensable ingredient in it.

Professor Emil Brunner's recent monumental work, *The Divine Imperative,*[49] cannot, strictly speaking, be included under any one of the preceding types of authoritarianism, though it is definitely authoritarian in cast. For Professor Brunner, the church as the " community of believers " rather than a hierarchical-sacramentarian mouthpiece of deity is an essential to the Christian faith which underlies Christian ethics; also he relies on the Scriptures but rejects as vicious the legalistic ethic based upon verbal inspiration; finally he comes closest to accepting the Friends' doctrine of inner light in his conception of revelation, which, to his mind, is the moment when the guidance of God is mediated to needy, sinful, hesitant man. Yet he carefully purges this last type of authority from any taint of individualism, insisting that the commandments of God have a universal validity which is discernible to the " community of believers." Dr. Brunner adds one other source of authority to these three. This is " God's action," which the believer encounters as he struggles

[49] New York: The Macmillan Co., 1937.

with his problems. This, to my mind, is almost sufficient ground for moving Brunner's "Protestant ethic" over into the category of an empirical religious ethic, since the ultimate validation of the insights born of church, Scriptures and revelation is to be found in ethical action. I have not so disposed of it because of the author's conviction that "ethics is only a section of dogmatics"[50] and that Christian dogmatics is fundamentally authoritative since it derives from the Word of God mediated through the Scriptures and revelation. His own words on this matter deserve quotation: "As for faith in general, so also for the good, it is true that God's Word is twofold: the Scripture and the Spirit, the unity between the Word that has taken place and the Word that is taking place now. The love of God revealed in Christ, in the Scriptures, is the same love of God which is shed abroad in our hearts by the same life-giving Spirit."[51]

Precisely what help, then, is Christian ethics to the Christian who is confronting a moral problem? In the first place it confronts him with the fact that "God only demands one thing: that we should live in his love,"[52] which love is mediated to the believer by the fellowship in the faith, through Scripture, and through revelation personally received yet shareable with other Christians. Then, getting down to the spade work of ethical action, Brunner affirms that ethics "can prepare the decision of the individual as carefully as a conscientious legal adviser prepares the decision of the judge by the most careful consideration of all possibilities."[53] Then the individual must choose. But the wisdom of his choice rests with "the free action of God,"[54] whose will and way

[50] *Ibid.*, p. 152 (footnote).
[51] *Ibid.*, p. 92.
[52] *Ibid.*, p. 165.
[53] *Ibid.*, p. 139.
[54] *Ibid.*, p. 88.

can never be reduced to an ethical lawbook which contains all the answers.

In consequence we are prepared for Professor Brunner's flat assertion that there is no such thing as a " Christian " economic or social program. In all the five hundred and sixty-seven pages of the book, Christian ethics never gets closer to a concrete personal, social or moral problem than to emphasize that to the degree that we are Christians (essentially an authoritarian achievement) we shall know the correct thing to do. I cannot leave Brunner's thesis without observing that it is wholly unconvincing because of its uneven handling of the authority of revelation in the moment of choice and the free action of God manifest in the consequences based upon that choice. If the revelation mediated to the Christian in moral perplexity is authoritative, why should it ever be modified, much less repudiated by the free action of God? The whole emphasis of Brunner's book falls on the antecedents of ethical action rather than on the consequences, and since the deliverances of God are essentially authoritarian, Christian ethics, for Brunner, may correctly be styled a spirit-guided ethics.

The most that authority, be it church, Bible or conscience, can do is lend assistance to the direction of ethical action; it cannot coerce the details of empirical problems into its prescriptive patterns. Regulative principles, embodying values, are essential to the solution of concrete cases, but, as was pointed out in an earlier chapter, the unfinished, dynamic nature of empirical reality keeps judgments of relevance within the area of probability. This is so far from being an empty logical form that recognition of it is the dividing line between authoritarian ethics on the one side and empirical ethics on the other.

Since authoritarian religious ethics has been unable to fulfill its high promise of being an infallibly sure guide in ethical action, we shall now assess the difficulties faced by an ethics proceeding along empirical lines yet deriving its regulative principles from religion. Whereas the former essayed guaranteeing an infallible choice, the most the latter hopes for is intelligent choosing. No one would spend time with the latter were the former available, but such is not the case. Bishop Francis J. McConnell writes, " Almost all Christianity's difficulties come of trying to make word flesh. The word may be permanent but flesh changes." [55] Authoritarianism has been unable to bring the incarnation to pass by decree (a mode of creativity perhaps wisely reserved for God alone), but its efforts are far from futile, since its various bases continually reappear as reservoirs of the seminal ideas of every known form of empirical religious ethics.

EMPIRICAL RELIGIOUS ETHICS

The empirical approach to moral problems is based upon a clear perception of the area of uncertainty in which the authoritative principle is coupled to concrete cases. It asserts that ethical action stands a good chance of being thoroughly vicious unless the hazardous nature of this uncertainty is fully recognized and reduced to a minimum by careful handling of the crucial factors involved. It is therefore profoundly suspicious of the minor premise of the ethical syllogism whereby authoritarian ethics seeks to prescribe an infallible choice for particular problems; for the minor premise claims to subordinate the specific problem under a general category dealt with in the major premise. An empirical religious ethic endeavors to mediate between regulative principles or

[55] *Christendom*, Autumn, 1935, p. 185.

ideals and specific problems which can be solved only by application of some regulative principle, by following the leading of some ideal regarded as relevant. Although it disclaims the prescriptive intentions of authoritarian ethics, it does not repudiate the ethical principles espoused by the latter. Rather, we may lay it down as a general rule that all forms of empirical religious ethics make constant use of some one or more of the traditional sources of authority.[56] It accepts their ideals as relevant principles of action, but insists that one cannot tell prior to their eventuation as consequences whether, or to what extent, they are really relevant to the problem at hand. This is the exact operation in which tentativeness and certainty must be kept in supplementary working relations if constructive ethical action is to result. This position, of course, is worlds removed from ethical nihilism, in which one ideal is as good as another, since it regards the moral ideals of good and right as phantasies born of despair rather than as approximations of the nature of the value structure of the universe. An empirical religious ethic is differentiated from such thought by its belief in the existence of a value structure and by the constant use it makes of the most acute observations and reflections upon past experience that are available and accepts them as safe guides in present perplexities.

The form of ethics we are now considering has a full-bodied respect for the complex, dynamic character of every moral problem — a complexity which defies complete classification and analysis, a dynamic quality which realizes itself in continuing activity. It accepts as elemental fact Dewey's twin assertions that "all action is an invasion of the future, of the unknown. Conflict and uncertainty are ultimate

[56] Inge, *op. cit.*, chaps. 1 and 2.

traits," [57] and that " the moral issue concerns the future. . . . It is prospective; . . . the moral problem is that of modifying the factors which now influence future results." [58] Accepting this analysis of the metaphysics of the (any) moral problem, an empirical religious ethics believes intelligent choosing among alternate possibilities to be the *summum bonum* of ethical action. It uses ideals and principles born of traditional authorities as suggestive rather than mandatory.

Should the query be raised, In what sense can such an ethic be called religious? a twofold answer may be made. (1) It is religious if and to the extent that it derives its ideals and regulative principles from some phase of religious tradition. (2) It is religious in so far as it recognizes the existence of a value structure encountered in the life process, of which ideals are approximations and to which they are answerable, through consequences of action under their guidance, for their validity. An empirical religious ethic, therefore, emphasizes (1) the relevance of ideals to moral problems, (2) the possibility of discovering, through ethical exploration, the fuller nature of the value structure of the universe, (3) the necessity of personal commitment to the value structure of the universe if ideals are to impregnate action sufficiently to control it, yet are to be held subject to modification in the light of the discoveries born of ethical action. Each of these merits closer attention, since in all we shall discern the polar relationship of tentativeness and certainty and see the truth of an earlier assertion that ethical action depends upon the careful preservation of this relationship.

1. The Relevance of Ideals to Moral Problems. An empirical religious ethic can answer with an emphatic affirmative the initial query of this chapter: Can the ideal defined

[57] *Human Nature and Conduct*, p. 12.   [58] *Ibid.*, pp. 18–19.

as an instrument of discovery command sufficient loyalty to evoke ethical action? I am taking it for granted that we need not pause for a lengthy argument over the importance of ideals. It ought to be self-evident that they are essential to ethical action, because they are human perceptions and articulations of values and their meaning for existence. Without judgments of value, of better and worse, good and bad, embedded in ideals, there can be no evaluation of action. Professor F. C. Sharp writes: "The source of all judgments upon conduct, both judgments of right and judgments of good, is certain ideals. . . . An ideal is a force, it tends to produce action in conformity with itself. These ideals are thus not merely the source of our judgment, but also the foundation of the moral life." [59] Dr. Clifford Barrett concurs: "Ideals are the patterns and goals of man's world. They constitute the architectural plans according to which he constructs conduct and institutions. Theirs is a dynamic as well as a normative function. They present that which is to be attained, and man, appreciating the value to be derived from the attainments they suggest, feels an urge to accomplish their fulfillment." [60]

The ideal is essential to ethical action, because it endeavors to guide man into a fuller relationship with the value structure of the universe. Therefore it is neither a luxury nor a phantasy, though some ideals frequently partake of the character of both. And it is more than a rigid summary of past experience. Professor Dewey argues the matter in this way: "Every ideal is preceded by an actuality; but the ideal is more than a repetition in inner image of the actual. It projects in securer and wider and fuller form some good which

[59] *Ethics* (New York: Century Co., 1928), p. 493.
[60] *Ethics* (New York: Harper & Bros., 1933), p. 120.

has been previously experienced in a precarious, accidental, fleeting way." [61] I take this to mean that the ideal drives its roots into past experiences of value which have been precious but fragmentary. The function of the ideal, then, is to generalize upon such experiences, to depict them in cosmic terms, to see in them clues to a fuller, richer value structure than anything yet dreamed of. They become an atmosphere in which man lives, moves, hopes and works. Professor N. Hartmann points out that " the living values of all moral systems find their most effective, most satisfactory embodiment in concrete ideals, whether these be only free creations of the phantasy or be borrowed from living examples." [62]

I doubt whether we can find many examples of values being effectively nurtured by ideals that are " free creations of the phantasy." Newell Dwight Hillis somewhere suggests one when he writes that " one hundred years after Homer wrote the *Iliad* ninety thousand young Achilles' trod the soil of Greece." Aesop's fables, the various mythologies, fairy stories, may be what Dr. Hartmann has in mind, but I suspect that all such rely heavily upon definite socio-cultural patterns for their moral maxims and are scarcely " free creations." Popular ideals, always projected upon great persons and projects, are effective depictions of the values cherished by the people. Thus Washington symbolizes integrity; Lincoln, magnanimity; Theodore Roosevelt, activity; Wilson, peace. The great projects of any age literally bristle with folk ideals; witness the age of the Crusades in which the romantic ideals of chivalry and the religious ideals of service of, obedience to, and humility before the will of God shared popular approval. For a period following the World War the League of Nations and the World Court were projects

[61] *Human Nature and Conduct*, p. 23.   [62] *Ethics*, I, 198.

which embodied the ideal of peace for our day. When confidence in them began to slip, the Kellogg-Briand Peace Pact outlawing war became the new embodiment for many. Now that our confidence in it is running out, we are searching for a new bearer of the ideal. Disillusionment is rife because we have been unable as yet to discover one, and until we do action for peace is going to seem far-fetched and pointless. All of which illustrates the single point that ideals are essential to ethical action, and that they never remain simply concepts, but tend to invest themselves in persons and projects through which they control action.

Hartmann insists that ideals or principles are manifestations of the dynamic nature of moral values, and his analysis of the relationship between moral values and existence is clear and convincing. Though, according to his metaphysics, moral values have an ideal self-existence — that is, inhere in the realm of ideal being — they are never perceived by man as wholly neutral entities. When beheld they are always in the category of " ought-to-be," and this translates itself into man's ethical consciousness as " ought-to-do." [63] Moral values, then, actually intersect the area of existence in the form of ideals or principles which struggle to insert the order of the value into existential reality. " It belongs to their [values'] essence as principles of the ethos [of man] that they transcend the sphere of essentialities and of ideal self-existence and seize hold on the fluctuating world of moral acts. They must be principles of the actual ethical sphere also." [64]

Whether we view them instrumentally with Dewey or metaphysically with Hartmann, we arrive at the single conclusion that ideals can be trusted as guides in moral perplexity. They are ethical instruments through which values born

[63] *Ibid.*, pp. 233 ff.   [64] *Ibid.*, p. 236.

of experience endeavor to previse and control action in the face of moral problems. This is not to praise them overmuch; they too must meet such problems in the area of uncertainty. Ideals never furnish us with all we know or need to know for infallible choices. To put it pictorially, ideals are to moral problems what a compass is to a mariner, giving a sense of direction, but telling nothing of the conditions of sailing, depth of water, etc., which are equally, but no more, important to a successful voyage.

An empirical Christian ethic will strive to solve moral problems by means of the ideal of love which it feels most adequately relates man to the value structure of the universe. Needless to say this has resulted in all sorts of interpretations of love, all of which intend to bring it closer to the realities of moral problems. Dean W. R. Inge and Dr. Reinhold Niebuhr represent respectively liberal and radical interpreters of an empirical Christian ethic. It is therefore germane to our purpose to scrutinize their understanding and use of the ideal of love.

Dean Inge speaks of " love which as a philosophical principle means that we are members one of another, so that the welfare of all is the good of each." [65] He both bolsters and clarifies this statement by taking the life and teachings of Jesus as " regulative principles." These lead him to describe " love to God " as comprising " the consciousness of deep dependence, the sentiment of devout gratitude, and the conviction that the love and the presence of God surround us like an atmosphere." [66] Love of man he describes in this way: " Christian love is the recognition of a fact — the brotherhood of humanity in Christ, involving a claim — that in all things we should seek the highest good of our neighbor, as if his

[65] *Op. cit.*, p. 25.   [66] *Ibid.*, p. 43.

good were our own." [67]   Dean Inge then proceeds to take up
a series of crucial ethical problems drawn from social and personal life and endeavors to elucidate the meanings of love in
terms of each perplexity.   Insisting as he does that " civilization . . . is actually passing into a new phase," [68] one with
which the experience of the past is unable to cope, he seeks
to get a true picture of each problem by availing himself of
statistics, reports, opinions, and an amazing number of other
interpretations, in terms of which he endeavors to state the
meaning of ethical action guided by the Christian ideal of
love.   And the ideal of love does introduce a sense of direction
into the problem, a consciousness of " oughtness "; yet there
is always room for debate over his specific recommendations.
The crucial point in such debate is always over whether love
means exactly this or something else.   Facts and faith are
not always as congenial as the lion and the lamb are going
to be — some day.   An uneliminable margin of inconclusive-
ness hems in the author's conclusions in each problem.

Dr. Niebuhr holds that Jesus' conception of love is fundamental to Christian ethics and is the source of hope and despair alike.   " Jesus' conception of pure love is related to the
idea of justice as the holiness of God is related to the goodness
of men.   It transcends the possible and the historical." [69]   But
it is not wholly unrelated to existence.   It is operative in our
developing theories of justice, for example.   " No absolute
limit can be placed upon the degree to which human society
may yet approximate the ideal [of forgiving love].   But it
is certain that every achievement will remain in the realm
of approximation.   The ideal in its perfect form lies beyond
the capacities of human nature." [70]   Hence love earns the

---

[67] *Ibid.,* pp. 43–44.
[68] *Ibid.*

[69] *Op. cit.,* p. 31.
[70] *Ibid.,* p. 111.

startling title of " impossible possibility." [71]   Although " love perfectionism " is not feasible in our world of relative goods and values — indeed may be vicious if taken as literally applicable to our problems — it continues to be the star by which the Christian sets the course of his ethical action. He will plunge into the relativities of existence and devote his energies toward securing a greater degree of justice; he will, in short, be guided by an alert ethic of compromise (almost a " prudential ethic," which Dr. Niebuhr scorns) rather than be numbed into apathetic, if not dangerous, inaction by an absolutistic ethic which will have love or nothing. Yet even the relativistic ethics which Dr. Niebuhr champions as being the only one suitable to the realities of existence derives its significance from the fact that it is an approximation of what he calls ideal love.[72] Its light is borrowed light.

Needless to say, I have no serious quarrel with Dr. Niebuhr's penetrating thesis; it is far too excellent and convincing a portrayal of the meaning of tentativeness and certainty in ethical action for me to do other than acclaim it. Love, for him, is a definite, dynamic value structure operative in degree within existence, yet in its absolute nature wholly transcendent to the relativities of life. Christian ethics gets its direction from " pure love," then settles down to the grim, desperate task of moving personal and social life toward perfection by means of immediate goals which are admittedly approximations.[73]

Ideals, then, not only are relevant to moral problems but represent an indispensable ingredient of any satisfactory way

[71] *Ibid.*, pp. 117 ff.

[72] " Ideal love," as Dr. Niebuhr uses it, is synonymous with what I have been calling " value structure."

[73] The ethical thought of John Oman, *Natural and Supernatural,* and F. R. Barry, *Christianity and the Modern World,* makes this same point.

of dealing with them. Ideals are not ultimates — but they are approximations of a value structure which is ultimate and which finally judges the activity incited by ideals in its name. Ideals are not confident masters of every moral perplexity, since the complexity of such problems defies exhaustive analysis — but by emphasizing as supreme the values seen to be involved in the problem they do provide a sense of direction which action should take if these values are to be preserved and furthered. Since ideals are conditioned not alone by our limited past experience, but also by our interpretations of that and all other experience thought to be relevant; since they gain their specific actional content from our analysis of the complexity of the problem at hand; since they so easily become sentimental clichés — for these reasons, ideals are not to be worshiped nor even treated with awe. They are tools with which the religious person works as he strives to insert his religious insights into the stuff of existence, and are in constant need of attention if they are to serve him well. But they are his best tools and are therefore not to be treated lightly. Without them, religion is an ethical luxury.

2. *The Possibility of Discovering the Fuller Nature of God through Ethical Action.* An empirical Christian ethic never loses sight of the fact that it is a religious enterprise. Dean Inge rightly warns us that " the ethics of Christianity are religious ethics; they have their center in God." [74] That the presuppositions of religion seriously complicate ethical theory is avowed by Hartmann, who sees in them several indissoluble antinomies which even his brilliant, subtle mind cannot resolve.[75] Dr. Niebuhr admits the difficulty since secular ethics may talk of error, whereas religious ethics speaks of sin; secular ethics speaks of progress, religious ethics of holy

[74] *Op. cit.,* p. 4.   [75] *Op. cit.,* III, chap. 21.

love. This is unavoidable, since religion introduces the "dimension of depth" [76] into life and ethical thought. A religious ethic, therefore, regards its ideals and concepts as valid if, and to the degree that, they express the nature of fundamental reality. It is well to remind ourselves that a religious ethic has a confidence in the future which secular ethics neither can nor desires to claim, in that the truth or error of its precepts will be determined by the continuing activity of God. It accepts as profoundly true Schiller's assertion that "the history of the world is the judgment of the world." [77] It is because the Christian religion believes in a "living" [78] rather than a "dead" or absentee God, and in an "unfinished" [79] rather than a completed universe, that its ethics provides the central thread of ethical theorizing in the Western world even to this day. Christian ethics sees a victory for religious insight in its defeats and a source of religious joy in its failures, for "hath not the Lord spoken?"

Ethical action is the most inclusive religious experience open to man. In it, past experience conditions present action in order to control in some measure at least future results. Insights, reasons, experiences garnered all the way from antiquity to modernity and harvested from the lives of others as well as self — all these humbly await the judgment of God as they guide human action into the future. Rationalist and mystic alike must finally bow before the prophetic summation of religious living: "By their fruits shall ye know them." And the only fruits known to man are in the area of action, understanding this to mean something other than a scurry-

[76] Niebuhr, op. cit., p. 4.
[77] Quoted by Brunner, Our Faith (New York: Charles Scribner's Sons, 1936), p. 146.
[78] Moehlman's phrase.
[79] T. S. Gregory's phrase.

ing hither and yon; to mean in fact profound interaction with others with mutuality or love as the ideal controlling the process.

The philosopher of religion lends a hand to an empirical religious ethic which seeks to discover God through ethical action. He clarifies crucial concepts and ideals, examines assumptions, and strives to heighten the unity of the cognitive equipment. The theologian also is indispensable, since he aids the philosopher not alone by introducing the support of tradition, wherever possible, but also by relating the fruits of his reflections to the fact of human need. The mystic contributes his offering of warm personal communion with God. But all must always remember, and ought to rejoice in the fact, that all such definitions, interpretations and visitations must return for validation to the actional sphere whence they sprang. Dean Inge felt the truth of this when he included among the closing sentences of his book this one: "The church, like a wise householder, must bring out of her treasure things new and old, as new things that are the legitimate interpretation of the original gospel for a state of society of which the first Christians never dreamed, and old things upon which the illuminating Spirit has passed with quickening breath and revealing light." [80]   Yet whether these treasures are really treasures only time and experience, perhaps bitter, can tell.

3. Commitment to God as the Enduring Incentive to Ethical Action.[81] The supreme loyalty of the Christian must be to God rather than to any ideals, however precious. Only if this is so can he be an effective champion of ideals. For the

[80] *Op. cit.,* p. 420.
[81] Cf. Gregory Vlastos, *The Religious Way* (New York: Association Press, 1934), for a thorough discussion of commitment.

spotlight of need does shift from one ideal to another in accordance with human need. Freedom will be to one generation what peace is to another and security to a third. Any given generation needs all three, but in the confused course of human events they usually have been fought for singly rather than collectively. Any empirical religious ethics worth the name will strive to orient individual and society alike to the pressing moral perplexities of the day. This, as we have been noting, requires paying strict attention to compelling ideals or regulative principles of action. Although religious faith comes to a burning focus in ethical action, it is never exhausted in it. For through ethical activity religious faith seeks a fuller understanding of, a firmer grasp on, the value structure of the universe. Its beliefs regarding God, man and the good life, nurturing as they do the ideals which govern ethical action, come into immediate contact with the reality whose nature they are attempting to describe or interpret to men.

Through ethical action, then, God speaks to man — accepting, modifying or repudiating the ideals and their parent beliefs. The pragmatic keynote of prophetic religion, namely, that God speaks through his works, is fundamental to an empirical religious ethic. Obviously there is much of sheer faith in this view — a standing on the springboard of the partially known and partially experienced and plunging therefrom into what is regarded as the essential nature of reality.

Thus the Christian religion injects the ideal of love into all moral issues, neither because we possess exhaustive evidence that it is the ultimate nature of reality nor because we can specify exactly what its implications are for concrete issues, but because it, better than any other, sums up the life and teachings of Jesus, the ethical thrust of the movement these evoked, and the experiences of value encountered by all who strive to follow them. Christian theology, implemented by a theory of value which recognizes God's continuing activity as the ultimate fact, gathers into a coherent form our experiences of value and sees therein evidence of the love of God. Christian worship, utilizing this in its effort to convince man that without God he is lost and with God he is saved, leads man to the frontier of the known and bids him gather his energies and insights together if he would walk with God into the future. Christian ethics leads man into that future, supplying a sense of direction which enables him to feel his way through moral perplexities which otherwise would completely baffle him. Commitment to God, the value structure of the universe, the supreme value whose nature illuminates, some radiantly others faintly, the values encountered in daily life — this supreme loyalty is open to the Christian. To the degree that it characterizes his life he seeks in the multiple and complex problems of his day that mutuality, that oneness with his comrades and with God which when discovered can only be revered as holy.

TENTATIVENESS AND CERTAINTY IN ETHICAL ACTION

The polar relationship between tentativeness and certainty is aptly portrayed in the necessary yet provisional role of ideals or regulative principles in ethical action. The moral problems with which ethical action concerns itself are the most complicated of all problems. The most assiduous investigation may neglect major relevant factors. Usually the compulsion to act is so pressing that the deliberate analytical approach is difficult. One thing however is clear: precious values are at stake and can be rescued only by decisions and actions based upon a perception of their plight and designed to release and further them.

The metaphysics of ethical action can be described in this way: Lying in concentric circles about the concrete moral problem, and in approximately this relationship, are (1) alternate choices, (2) the ideal, (3) theological beliefs (beliefs about value and human nature), (4) attitude of devotion to God (consciousness of or reverence for value), (5) God (the value structure of the universe).

The ideal brings our past thought about and experience of God to bear upon the problem at hand. In this sense, then, the ideal is definitely a priori and enters the crisis clothed with logical as well as psychological certainty. It is the direction-finder in moral confusion, but it does not thereby furnish all relevant facts about the perplexity, neither can it establish, *prior to action under its guidance,* its own relevance to the situation. We will hold ideals tentatively, then, in proportion to the purity and strength of our devotion to God. In ethical action ideals that have survived the proving grounds of past experience are put on the highways, byways and detours of life, and our confidence in them awaits confirmation. When weaknesses show up, as they inevitably do, we can remedy them, may even fashion a new vehicle and try once more; and do it with the joy reserved for those who face outward on the frontiers of life. Our devotion to God need not waver at any moment in this process. Steadfast devotion brings beliefs and ideals into being as attempts to articulate our fragmentary experiences of God. When these beliefs and ideals are proved inadequate, devotion brings forth other and sounder ones based upon that experience.

Ethical action, then, is the supreme moment in Christian experience, for in it we lay our beliefs, ideals and ideas on the altar of God, confident that he will accept, reject or modify them, and that we shall be enriched by a fuller knowledge of him.

INDEX

Abélard, 14, 119
Absolute: practical, 54
Abundant life: and institutions, 148 f.; definition of, 170
Adoration: and worship, 2 f.
Alexander, S., 26, 45, 139, 140 n.
Ames, E. S., 54 n.
Amos, 192 n.
Aquinas, Thomas, 13, 28, 35, 56, 119, 133, 134, 138
Archimedes, 75–76
Aristarchus of Samos, 36
Aristotle, 11, 29, 35, 57, 61–62, 138
Arminius, 147
Arnold, Matthew, 15
Aubrey, E. E., 18 n., 22 n., 27 n., 29 n.
Augustine, 12, 13, 56, 119, 133, 147, 163, 206
Authority: in Christian ethics, 197 ff.; weakness of, 213 f.
Ayres, C. E., 17 n.

Babson, Roger, 6
Bacon, Francis, 14, 15, 16, 56
Bacon, Roger, 119
Baptism: growth of symbol, 177 f.
Barrett, Clifford, 217
Barry, F. R., 22, 25, 222 n.
Barth, Karl, 19, 20 n.
Barthian, 5, 20, 147
Bartlet, J. V., 179
Belief: religious, Chap. VII *passim;* as approximation to reality, 108 ff.; as revelation of reality, 102 ff.; conceptions of, 98 ff.
Bennett, John, 192 n., 194
Bergson, Henri, 16, 87, 96, 139
Bernard of Clairvaux, 119

Bernhardt, W. H., 100, 119 n.
Boutroux, E., 16, 84, 87–88
Bowne, Borden Parker, 139
Brahe, Tycho, 36
Bridgman, P. W., 17, 68
Broad, C. D., 73, 76
Brown, W. A., 37, 49, 51, 105–8, 111 n.
Brunner, Emil, 20 f., 211–13, 224 n.
Buddhism, 135
Burtt, Edwin A., 43, 54, 107
Butler, Bishop, 55

Cadman, W. H., 163 n.
Calvin, 133, 147, 186, 206
Case, S. J., 133
Cave, Sydney, 28
Celebration: and worship, 166 f.; in primitive religion, 166 f.
Certainty: definition of, 32–33 ff.; logical, 35 ff.; psychological, 33 ff.; of conclusion, 37 ff.; of method, 39 ff.; historical positions, 1 ff.; need of, 2 ff.; possibility of, 32
Christ: central Christian symbol, 176, 183 f.; doctrines of, 149 ff.
Clement, 179
Cohen, Morris, 33, 42–44, 64
Commitment: to God, 225 f.
Concept: analysis of, 67 ff.
Conscience: and mysticism, 208 f.; as authority in ethics, 205 ff.
Contingency: Chap. VI *passim;* and knowledge, 79 ff.; and natural law, 87 ff.; and scientific method, 83 ff.; as ignorance, 78 f.; definition of, 57 f., 78; of past, 94; of future, 94
Cooley, C. H., 140 n.
Copernicus, 36

231

114985

Oman & Janssen, 22 - 25

— Summary statement.